CASTLE CARY AND ANSFORD
TIME TO REFLECT

Castle Cary's most famous structure provides an eminently suitable backdrop for PC Geoffrey Laver, who was posted to the town in 1947 in succession to PC R. Garland. His career began in 1934 in Taunton with subsequent postings to Weston-super-Mare, Yeovil and Crewkerne. Popular and greatly respected in Castle Cary, on his retirement in 1964 after 17½ years of service, he was presented with an inscribed album and a suite of furniture. His outside interests included the Castle Cary Produce Association, of which he was a successful exhibitor, and membership of Castle Cary Youth Advisory Committee. The Round House was built in 1779 at a cost of £23, appropriated from benefactions for the poor, as a temporary lock-up. It replaced a tree standing on the site, and although evidently little used, survived all suggestions that it might be removed. In 1922 the Lord of the Manor, Sir Henry Hoare, gave the building to the Parish Council and restoration work has secured its future.

CASTLE CARY AND ANSFORD
TIME TO REFLECT

THE LIVING HISTORY GROUP

When so many trifles steal away the hours, reflection should surely be allowed its moments: wishing frequently to introduce such pleasures, this volume is respectfully dedicated to every reader.

First published in 2002

© Living History Group, Castle Cary

Dickins Printers, Castle Cary · 01963 350110

Setting and page layout:
TypeStyle, Yeovil · 01935 429403

ISBN 1 902247 01 9

CONTENTS

Preface & Introduction *1*

Ansford *7*

Castle Cary *19*

Weather *49*

Agriculture *53*

Industries *63*

Trades and Businesses *79*

Schools and Childhood *91*

Churches *99*

Wartime *107*

Personalities *113*

Public Services *121*

Transport *129*

Sports *135*

Events *145*

Carnivals *163*

Curiosities *171*

Further Reading *177*

PREFACE

A photographic celebration of Castle Cary and Ansford's past was the object of an exhibition held by the Living History Group in the Possi Gallery during June 2000 as part of the town's millennium celebrations. Not only did a considerable number of visitors view the displays, but the exhibition also generated considerable interest in the publication of a selection from the material collected by the Group, with the advantage of expanded explanatory captions. This book is the result.

The members of the Living History Group responsible for the compilation of the book are as follows:-

RAYMOND BOYER was born in Castle Cary and educated locally. He was one of the first pupils to attend the new Ansford Secondary Modern School, and has been engaged in agriculture for his entire life. He was a member and later Chairman and Club Leader of the Mid-Somerset Young Farmers' Club, and also a member and for a time Chairman of Yeovil and District N.F.U. Always involved in the local community, he has served as a member of Castle Cary Town Council for over 30 years.

Ray and his wife Olive have two sons, David in Namibia and Philip in Dorset. Ray was a founder member of the Living History Group and has acted as Chairman since it was founded. Olive is President of the Group.

NORMAN DILL was born in 1925, the second son of George and Ellen Dill, and was educated at the Public Elementary School (now Castle Cary Primary School). He has lived in Castle Cary all his life, with the exception of his service (after a short period in the Home Guard), with the Royal Artillery during the Second World War as a driver, in France, Belgium and Germany. Employment as a postman for thirty four years enabled him to accumulate a considerable fund of knowledge about the town, and since his retirement in 1985 he has devoted many hours each week as a steward in the Museum in the Town Hall. He is also a sidesman at All Saints Church, and a keen member of the local Gardening Club.

Sadly Norman passed away on 7th February 2002 during the final stages of the preparation of this book. He had been a member of the Living History Group since its inception, and had always played a full and enthusiastic part in all its activities. In spite of the difficulties occasioned by the progress of his illness he continued to assist the Group until a few weeks before his death, and only then asking, like Captain Oates, to be excused for a while. He will be greatly missed, not only by the members of the Group, but also by the community which he served for so long.

RUTH LODGE was born at Ditcheat in 1932 and spent her childhood at Wyke Champflower and attended schools in Lamyatt and Bruton. She moved to Castle Cary in 1944, and attended Ansford Secondary Modern School. On leaving school she trained as a cheesemaker, but after her marriage in 1953 became a cook, spending many years at the George Hotel, and latterly, prior to her retirement, at South Cary House.

BRIAN LUSH, aged 45, has lived in Castle Cary his entire life, and is the third generation of his family to do so. He has seven siblings, his father Edwin has six, and his grandfather Reginald had twenty. The Lush connection with Castle Cary began when his great-grandfather Eli, born at Bayford, near Wincanton, moved to Galhampton as a 14-year-old apprentice to Mr. Bartlett, a farmer and butcher, in 1871, before starting a butchery business in Castle Cary in 1888, which was transferred to the present High Street shop in 1894. From these premises the family have been serving the community for 108 years. Brian continues the family's trade. He is especially interested in local history and that of his family, and has amassed a considerable photographic collection. He joined the Living History Group in 2000.

JULIEN NICHOLLS was born in 1936 at Bridgwater, moving with his family to Evercreech in 1939. He was educated at Evercreech Church Primary School and Ansford Secondary Modern School, followed by National Service in the Royal Air Force re-fuelling aircraft in Germany and Cyprus during the Suez Crisis of 1956. Most of his working life was spent in Street and Castle Cary as a buyer of raw materials for various departments of Strode/Avalon Components, a division of Clarks Shoes Ltd. He has lived in Castle Cary since his marriage to Valerie in 1960. Always having a keen interest in local history, he was pleased to become a member of the Living History Group when it was formed in 1995.

VALERIE NICHOLLS was born at Castle Cary and educated at Miss Grosvenor's School, Castle Cary Junior School and Ansford Secondary Modern School. The greater part of her working life was spent in the employment of Mr. T. M. Trowbridge at his drapery and outfitting shop in Fore Street. She has been a member of the Living History Group since its formation in 1995. During her lifetime she has witnessed many changes in Castle Cary and Ansford and now enjoys working with the Group in preserving records of various aspects of past and present life in the area, for the benefit of future generations.

ANNETTE PEARCE was educated at Northtown School for Girls in Taunton and later at Taunton Technical College. She moved to Castle Cary with her husband and young son in 1972, and worked at Haynes Publishers of Sparkford for eight years as a typesetter. She then spent three years working for a Chartered Surveyor in Shepton Mallet and a short spell at Woodforde & Drewett, Solicitors of Castle Cary, before obtaining employment with Cooper & Tanner, Chartered Surveyors, of Castle Cary, for whom she worked 17 years until retiring a few years ago. Castle Cary town and its people are of prime importance to her.

ADRIAN PEARSE was born in 1958, a grandson of Wosson John and Margaret Mary Carlyle (nee Hill) Barrett of Ansford, and a descendant of many generations of ancestors in Castle Cary. He was educated at Sexey's School, Bruton, and Keble College, Oxford, where he read Modern History. Currently a dairy farmer at East Pennard, he is an active, if controversial, figure in the local community, having served for 20 years as P.C.C. secretary, 15 years as Churchwarden, and also as a Parish Councillor, presently as Chairman. He is Chairman of the Board of Trustees for the parish charities. His many and varied interests include genealogy and local history: consequently he was honoured by the invitation to become Editor of Living History Group publications in 1998, and has undertaken the tasks involved in preparing this volume with alacrity.

JOHN PITMAN was born in South Street, Castle Cary, in 1934 and attended Castle Cary Infants and Junior School, and Ansford Secondary Modern School. He moved with his parents to Venus Cottage in 1939, and left school in 1949, then served his time as an apprentice carpenter and joiner in Bath, before returning to Castle Cary and employment with local builders. He married in 1957, and became self-employed in 1960. John played soccer and cricket for Castle Cary and has been a member of the Robins skittles team for 50 years. He served on Castle Cary Parish Council for eight years. His interests include sport and local history.

ANN SIMON was born and brought up in Surrey and educated at Sherborne School for Girls. She graduated from Nottingham University, where she read Social Administration, and moved to Castle Cary with her family in 1998. She has developed a career in human resources, and currently works as a Career Consultant. She has always had a keen interest in local history, and is one of the newest members of the Living History Group, joining after her third visit to the Millennium Photograph Exhibition, and therefore considers her contribution to be modest! She has never ceased to be amazed how wonderful a place Castle Cary is in which to live.

Newer members of the Group with the President. *Left to right*: Ann Simon; John Pitman; Olive Boyer (seated).

Members of the Living History Group outside the Possi Gallery with several display boards, June 2000.
Left to right: Adrian Pearse; Valerie Nicholls; Julien Nicholls; Brian Lush; Annette Pearce; Raymond Boyer; Norman Dill; Ruth Lodge; Simon Kenevan (of Possi Gallery).

The Living History Group acknowledges the substantial financial support received from South Somerset District Council, from the Awards For All Lottery Fund; the sponsorship of Wyvern Waste Ltd., towards the cost of providing a hard-back binding; and the assistance and encouragement of Paula and Simon Kenevan in staging the exhibition at the Possi Gallery, Castle Cary; as well as all those who have contributed their time, knowledge and material towards the fruition of this project, and especially the Cary 2000 Committee, proposer of the idea which set everything in motion.

INTRODUCTION

"The town hath little in it worthy commendation." So wrote Thomas Gerard in 1633. Castle Cary has come a long way in the centuries since he made this observation, and the collection of photographs presented here is an attempt to show just how much there is to admire in Castle Cary and Ansford. To fully appreciate them it is also necessary to paint in the background, to explain, and to illustrate, how the life and the landscape of the area has evolved. The photographic record over the last 150 years is considerable, but, alas, not fully comprehensive in terms of coverage. An attempt has been made, and it was no simple task, to select a balanced range of material providing as broad a spectrum of the life of these communities as possible. The result is the largest collection of images printed to date, a considerable proportion of which have not been previously published. Where this is not the case, the items selected are generally included because the publication in which they have appeared is no longer in print, or because they are old favourites, and most suitable for the task in hand. The oldest photographs are from the 1860s, but the vast majority date from the 1890s, through the golden age of the postcard, to the present day. Occasional printed ephemera has been included to provide period flavour.

What does the photographic record show us? Clearly Castle Cary has a fine architectural heritage. Its buildings may not be the most outstanding examples of their kind, but if one thinks of the term "local distinctiveness" then it is something of which Castle Cary has plenty. John Boyd's factory buildings and Donne's Higher Flax Mills were both prime examples of substantial Victorian construction, not built with simple utilitarian objectives, but as manifestations of confidence and substance, and with respect to aesthetic considerations as well. In this respect times have certainly changed. Castle Cary was by no means unique in this respect, one has only to look locally, for example, at the Clarks complex at Street, to see a similar pattern: it was very much an embodiment of the spirit of the age.

In domestic buildings too, Castle Cary has many fine examples. At one extreme is Florida House, flamboyant and resplendent at its elevated location, the quintessential mill owner's mansion. At the other are the smaller cottages, as seen from some of the earlier photographs, originally thatched, but again attractive examples of vernacular styles in their glowing warm Cary stone. With the coming of the railway, building materials could be cheaply procured from a wide area, and most thatch was replaced with clay tile and slate, and even though building design lost many of its local characteristics, Victorian detailing has produced many attractive and interesting features which blend well with the plainer and more formal Georgian facades.

The public buildings likewise show a care and attention to detail which adds immeasurably to the atmosphere of the town, so that the overall result is one of charm and character, which makes Castle Cary the special place it is. By being recognized, such characteristics can be preserved, and it is hoped that this book will, by drawing attention to many of these attractive and interesting features of the built environment, ensure that they are properly understood and their importance appreciated.

The other aspect portrayed in this volume is the life of the communities over the last century. Special occasions, sports and pastimes, trades and personalities are but some of the categories selected. It is hoped that many will find members of their family amongst these pages, but for those who do not, there is a record of how the communities have worked together, in times of peace and prosperity, and also in war and adversity. Over the years Castle Cary and Ansford have produced many individuals, even the odd notorious example, who have made an impact in their community or in an even wider area, and have influenced the evolution of the town as it is today. Castle Cary and Ansford are now thriving communities; a greater understanding of how they have become so can only be of benefit for the future. It is hoped that this book will provide a path in that direction.

An acrostic by Douglas Macmillan will serve as a fitting introduction to this collection.

A. V. Pearse, Editor

Castle Cary! Cary Castle! how the words like magic thrill
All the sons of all the homes that nestle there beneath the hill:
Still the pride of ancient effort beats within the local breast,
Though thy moat; and keep, and turrets, like their lords, have sunk to rest:
Low thy ramparts now are lying, and the gentle cattle graze
Even where the crash of battle thrilled thy lords in far-off days.

Castle Cary! Cary Castle! in the ends of earth to-day
Are thy sons and daughters mindful of their birth-spot far away:
Rural life perhaps is passing, and the love of some grows cold,
Yet thy glory hath foundations, and thy tale shall yet be told.

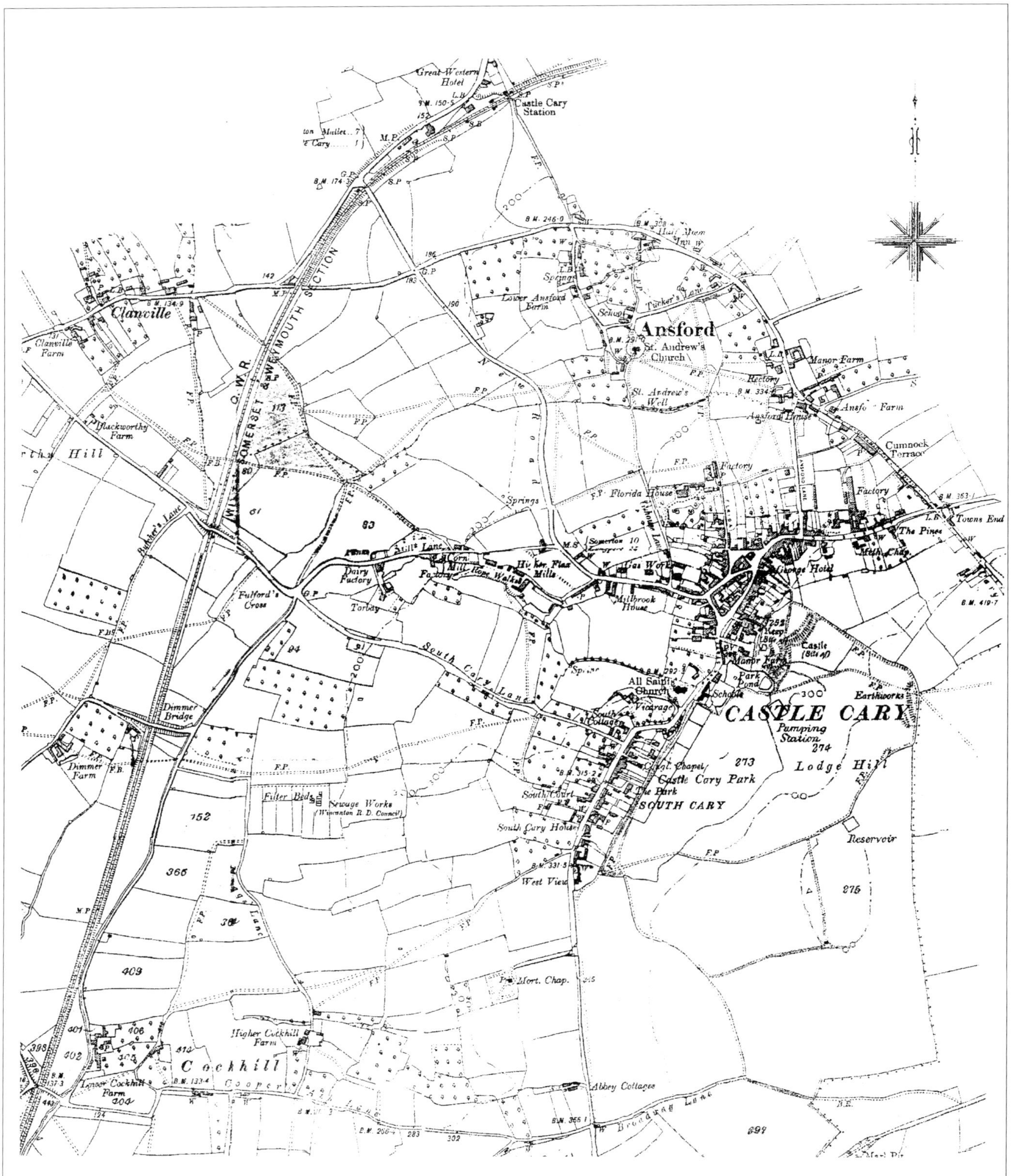

Castle Cary and Ansford 1903.

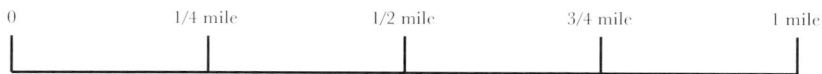

ANSFORD

ANSFORD INN (OLD COACHING INN)

During the 18th and early 19th century few inns in Somerset were better known than Ansford Inn. In addition to its importance to the coaching trade, the extensive premises hosted the County Ball, important meetings, auctions, etc, as well as providing a venue for cockfighting, bear-baiting and other pastimes of the era. The convivial atmosphere is well described, for example, in Parson James Woodforde's account of the Masquerade Ball held in 1767. The mother of the infamous Tucker was landlady in the 1740s. The Inn declined in importance from the 1850s with the decay of the coaching industry; the railways took passengers and replaced the stream of coal wagons which had provided an important trade. The building of the Market House in 1856, which contained a ballroom, resulted in the transfer of dances to these premises and a lingering decline ended with the surrender of the licence in 1879. Subsequently the main block was used as a furniture repository and saleroom by Messrs. Pither & Sons, and the outbuildings let to various tenants. The pillared porch was demolished by an army lorry during the Second World War and not re-built. In 1951 the premises were sold and have recently been sub-divided into residential apartments. The atmosphere of its golden age can be glimpsed from an inscription scratched on one of the windows. *(photo A. V. Pearse)*

> To Ansford Inn a traveller came,
> Chill'd through his universal frame,
> Into the kitchen straight he goes,
> First kiss'd the girl, then warm'd his nose.
> The Tea was good, the cream was sweet;
> The butter such as gods might eat;
> Full soon his blood its warmth regains,
> And capers nimbly through his veins;
> His horse and he refresh'd and gay;
> With wonted glee resumed their way.
> AW 1809

THE OLD PARSONAGE

The hand of time has fallen but lightly on the Old Parsonage at Ansford which exudes the atmosphere of the eighteenth century, even surrounded as it is by modern development.

The living of Ansford, together with that of Castle Cary, was held by the Woodforde family, themselves descended from an ancient and respectable family in Leicestershire, from 1719–1836. They were also Stewards of the Manors of Castle Cary and Ansford and representatives of the family were involved in many aspects of the life of the area for about 250 years.

It was at the Old Parsonage that the celebrated diarist, James Woodforde, was born in 1740 to Rev. Samuel Woodforde, Rector of Ansford and Vicar of Castle Cary. His mother Jane was the heiress of the Collins family of Ansford Manor House, often referred to as "The Lower House". James Woodforde's diary concerns itself with the minutiae of daily life, his social activities and the lives of those that entered his orbit. Events which at that time were changing the world do not concern him. Nothing better captures the feel of life in Castle Cary, Ansford, and the surrounding area at this time, and its perusal is strongly recommended.

James Woodforde lived at Ansford except for time spent at Winchester College and New College, Oxford, until becoming Curate at Thurloxton in 1763 and Babcary in 1764. He was ordained priest at Wells in 1764, and in 1765 became Curate of Castle Cary, giving up Babcary, and went to live at the "Lower House". He moved to the (Old) Parsonage in 1771 on his father's death, and continued as Curate of Castle Cary and Ansford until 1773. After a spell at New College, he returned to Ansford for a brief spell in 1776, before leaving for Weston Longeville, in Norfolk, as Rector. Here he remained until his death in 1803.

Another notable member of the Woodforde family was Samuel Woodforde (1764–1817) who became a member of the Royal Academy in 1807. Some of his works may be seen at Stourhead.

Alongside the Old Parsonage the road leading to the church is known as Tucker's Lane, commemorating the murder of Ansford resident Martha Tucker by her husband Reginald, with a hammer in 1775. He was tried in Wells and executed on Keward Green before an audience of 10,000; his body being later dissected at Langport.

The house as seen from the garden. *(photo Miss T. Rossiter)*

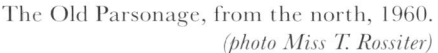

The Old Parsonage, from the north, 1960.
(photo Miss T. Rossiter)

The remaining fragment of Ansford's mediaeval cross, a portion of the shaft, was rescued from oblivion in 1904 by Rev. Price and set up, as shown here soon afterwards, on a new base situated on the west side of the churchyard. Such churchyard crosses were an important element in the mediaeval religious context and seem normally to have been positioned originally in front of and to the right of the principal south door of a church, but were often subsequently relocated. After the Reformation many were damaged or neglected, as appears to have been the case with Ansford's example. The remains of the Ansford cross were not observed by Charles Pooley in his survey of the old stone crosses of Somerset made in 1877, which makes its survival even more remarkable. *(photo K. Wright)*

A drawing made in 1902 of the cottages at the top of Ansford Hill where Charles Donne established his sailcloth manufacturing business in 1797 with the erection of about six looms. The inscribed stone in the wall marks the site of the death of Canon Longman. *(From postcard, A. V. Pearse collection)*

Buttwell House, on Ansford Hill, is seen here from a photograph taken in 1895, when it belonged to Reuben Newport, who had purchased the property at auction in 1880 for £325, including the two adjoining cottages, outbuildings and orchard. Beside the road in front of the house was a well, from which the property took its name, used by the occupants of all three houses and also the public. During the 1930s Buttwell was the home of Herbert Bliss, Reuben Newport's son-in-law, who was active in the Ansford community. Note the intricate Victorian cast iron porch, several examples of which were added to houses in Castle Cary and Ansford. *(photo Rev. A. Bliss)*

Only a portion survives of this thatched farmhouse from demolition in the early 1960s to make way for the present bungalows in Lower Ansford. Perhaps originally a long house, it possessed a cider house, barn and stable at either end, and was purchased by James Dauncey with the adjoining land from Henry Dyne in 1868, and passed via his son-in-law William Bettey to his four granddaughters, the last surviving of whom, Sarah Anna Bettey, lived here until shortly before her death in 1949, aged 96, after which the house was unoccupied. Around the front door grew an everlasting sweet pea; which in spite of the major disturbances of demolition and re-development of the site, survives to this day. The photograph dates from 1920.
(photo A. V. Pearse)

James Dauncey was born in the closing hours of 1793 at Barton-St-David and was a descendant of Joseph Dauncey, Rector of Keinton Mandeville 1686–1729, who had come thither from Wotton-under-Edge as a curate and married the daughter of the incumbent. The family originated as D'Anisy from Anisy in Normandy, where they were knights at the time of the Conquest. Other of the numerous descendants of Joseph were the Merrick family who had a shop at The Triangle in Castle Cary, and Miss Maidment, who ran a long established school at the Old Bank House in the High Street. The Daunceys of North Barrow and Hornblotton are also descendants. James farmed at Lydford, Sparkford and Arthur's Bridge, before he retired to Ansford in 1868, and died the following year. He was the Editor's great-great-great grandfather. *(photo A. V. Pearse)*

Ansford Manor House, a fine Elizabethan residence, was destroyed by fire in 1892 and subsequently largely demolished. Fragments of wall, the infilled cellars and some of the outbuildings survive, as do portions of the statues visible either side of the door. These, carved from blue lias, may be tomb effigies re-used after removal from a church, perhaps the previous Ansford church, and fragments remain recumbent on the wall opposite Laylocks in Lower Ansford, where this edifice formerly stood. Long in the possession of the Woodforde family, it was the residence of Parson James Woodford's feckless brother John and is frequently referred to in the former's diaries of the later 18th century. During the 19th century the property was the residence of Col. William Woodforde. The house and grounds contained his large collection of curiosities, including carved stonework, fossils, a whale bone arch and one of the two cannon used to celebrate the coronation of George III. Some of these items remain in the immediate locality. *(photo A. V. Pearse)*

Ansford Lodge remains unaltered from this view of 1890, recovered from a glass plate negative, though its surroundings have changed considerably, especially as a result of the construction of the access road to the Churchfield development in the 1970s. During the 18th century it was the home of the White family, relatives of the Woodfordes, then resident at The (Old) Parsonage. Indeed the signature of diarist James Woodforde's brother Heighes was scratched on a window pane here. *(photo N. Foster)*

The prosperity and stability of the decade before World War One is manifested in this group photograph of Ansford children taken on the Rectory Lawn.

Impeccably attired residents of Ansford pose for a photograph in the garden of Ansford Rectory in about 1909.
From left: back row: NK; Polly Ridout, George Taylor, Miss Francis; NK; Jim Lodge; Dorothy Taylor; Mark Green; Miss Francis; Revd Price. *Middle row:* Mrs (?) Skeels; NK; NK; NK. *Front row:* Walter Arnold; Alec Barnard; Arthur Arnold.

Ansford House, a substantial gentleman's residence, is said to have been built in the late 18th century for Dr James Woodforde, a relation of the diarist and a prominent figure in Castle Cary, also author of a noted treatise on dyspepsia. Dr James Clarke resided here in 1789, when John Wesley was his guest during a visit to Castle Cary. During the 1830s the house was occupied by Rev. Richard Warner, author of the major study 'A History of the Abbey of Glaston', who was often visited by his friend and fellow antiquarian, the acerbic Rev. John Skinner, perhaps the first to correctly speculate on the site of the castle. The house was extended to the south in the early 19th century by Messrs. Francis, when the whole property comprised three acres and in addition to extensive outbuildings, kitchen garden, orchards and paddock included Ansford Cottage and Ansford Villa, built in 1873 (now known as 'The Red House'). The process of dismemberment commenced soon after its sale in 1896 to Messrs. S. M. and W. Barrett, with the partition of Ansford Villa in 1905. Ansford Cottage was sold subsequently, and in the 1960s the orchard and paddock were developed for housing known as Coombe Close. The photograph shows the house in 1910. The central chimney has since been removed, otherwise the external appearance remains the same.

A lithograph of Hillcrest School, drawn by Paul M. Whiston in 1983. It was previously Ansford Rectory before being converted to a school during the 1950s. *(photo Mrs E. Churchouse)*

A view of Lower Ansford and its surroundings taken from the north in the early 1960s just before the Churchfields development linked the village core with Castle Cary, and the bungalows were constructed along Lower Ansford Lane. Clearly visible is the line of the former coach road winding up the hillside south of the station, replaced by Station Road in 1856 cutting across the original route to Clanville and the earlier field layout towards West Park. Field earthworks and ridge and furrow dating back to the mediaeval period and beyond are also apparent. *(photo A. V. Pearse)*

The children of Ansford gather outside Ansford Junior School on Coronation Day 12th May 1937 for King George VI and Queen Elizabeth. Included are: Sylvia Stockman; Joan Francis; Hazel Heathman; Marion Clothier; Vera Bleak; Sarah Barrett; Violet Lodge; Albert Lodge and Ronald Hicks. *(photo S. Garland)*

Lower Ansford Farm is seen here from the orchard opposite in 1937, decorated for the Coronation. It was later known as "The Orchards" and now as "The Old House". The irregular position of the windows indicates that the building is somewhat older than their design would indicate, and probably dates from the late 17th or early 18th century. The rendering was removed in the 1950s. The property was purchased by W. J. Barrett in 1935, who combined it with his aunt's land opposite and the buildings adjoining the site of Ansford Manor House. He farmed here until retirement in 1963, and moved to a bungalow built opposite. The house was sold to Miss Lewis, who later converted the adjoining cider house for residential use. Behind the house was an orchard with a gully alongside in which tradition asserts a fugitive was concealed during the Civil War period. It is thought that this was a male member of the Collins family, owners of the Manor House, sought by commonwealth troopers, perhaps in connection with the flight of Charles II after the battle of Worcester in 1651, who may have also hidden with him.
(photo A. V. Pearse)

A group outside "The Half Moon" at Ansford in the 1940s.
Left to right, front row: Eric Joyce (Landlord); Eileen Stockman.
Back row: Frank White; Mr. Chivers; Fred Cave; Bert Lodge; Gerald Cave. *(photo Ruth Lodge)*

The Sparkford Vale Harriers meet in front of the Brook House Inn (in Ditcheat parish) during the early 1960s. To the left are standing the Landlord Stanley Foster and his wife Mary. *(photo N. Foster)*

G. W. R. Station Castle Cary, and Creech Hill.— The Cornish express runs through this station at the rate of about 60 miles an hour. At the top of Creech Hill is a small encampment.

A view of the G.W.R. station from the west taken after the building of the line to Langport, constructed and opened in stages from 1903–1906. The station was opened on the 3rd September 1856, the first train being "The Mercury" running from Frome to Yeovil: the line reaching Weymouth in 1857. The line was originally a single track of broad gauge, converted to standard gauge in 1847 and doubled in 1881. Construction of the station involved re-routing the Ansford-Shepton Mallet road, which had previously passed roughly in the position of the present footbridge over the line, to the west, and building the present Station Road into Cary. Triumphal arches were erected for the reception of Lord Roberts at the station in 1901, and Buffalo Bill and the Wild West Show passed through enroute for Yeovil in 1903. The engine shed, parcels office and signal box were destroyed by German bombs on 3rd September 1942 and subsequently re-built. The Station Hotel was also destroyed, three were killed and ten injured. The chocolate and cream livery of the G.W.R. was finally erased during the 1960s, though a G.W.R. bench remains on the platform, the gas lamps removed and the waiting room on the south side of the line replaced with an architecturally inferior substitute c1980. Manual signalling had been superseded by this time. The station remains a thriving focus for commuter travel to London from a wide hinterland. *(photo A. V. Pearse)*

CASTLE CARY

Engravings or drawings of Castle Cary before the invention of photography are very rare. This engraving was made soon after the church was rebuilt in 1855 and shows the area now known as "The Triangle" looking very similar to its present appearance. Other versions of this view show a large Union flag over the Britannia Commercial Inn as it was then known.
(A. V. Pearse collection)

MARKET PLACE

For a considerable portion of its history, markets represented one of the primary functions of Castle Cary.

A charter had been granted by Edward IV to John de Zouche in 1468, by which a market might be held on Thursday in each week, with fairs on the eve, day, and morrow of St. Phillip and St. James' day, and of St. Margarets's day - May 1st and July 20th respectively. During the century or so which followed, this market apparently lapsed, for in 1614 a further charter was granted by King James I to the Earl of Hertford for a market within the town every Tuesday and a fair on the Thursday before Palm Sunday. In 1616 the markets were bought by Robert Devereux, Earl of Essex, and in this same year the first Market House was built.

Although there was at one time a flourishing sheep market in North Cary, on the site later occupied by Boyd's hair factory and the nurseries, the principal markets were held for many centuries either at the top or at the base of Bailey Hill, the latter site being formerly known as "The Cross" and now as "The Market Place". There is a tradition that a market cross once stood here (examples remain at Somerton, Cheddar and Shepton Mallet) which may have been demolished as a result of the construction in 1616 of the first Market House, or shortly afterwards. In spite of the decline of this latter building's market related functions, the market thrived - a newspaper of 1809 refers to Cary market as "one of the best in the West of England ... there being nearly 600 head of cattle numbered".

Four fairs annually were also held, the occasions which became established being: the Tuesday before Palm Sunday; the first of May; Whit-Tuesday; and the Tuesday after the 19th of September. The first of these was popularly known as "Little Weaving Tuesday", because the serge and dowlais makers largely abandoned their occupations and made merry on that day, and the last as "Gibbet Fair" in memory of the execution of Jack White in 1730.

Markets were held every other Tuesday, until by order of the Board of Agriculture they were moved to a new market yard in the "Brittannia" paddock at Millbrook opened on 18th March 1913.

A maypole was erected on "The Cross" in earlier times, the last occasion in about 1835, and "single stick" was played here until 1846. The Market House, erected in 1855, provided improved facilities, but failed to realise expected profits for its shareholders, and much of the ground floor area became used for storage of farm machinery and equipment sold by T. White, until fairly recent times.

The essence of Castle Cary's prime function is captured in this view of the market in 1906. Note the (quite sophisticated) hay making machinery, the cattle herded by boys in front of the Market House, the farmers in the background and the open drain running down the middle of the area. The same scene, with different buildings and costumes, would have typified this site in the Middle Ages. *(photo A. V. Pearse)*

The Market House serving its intended purpose and surrounded by the market on a Tuesday in 1906.

MARKET HOUSE

The Market House stands on the site of an earlier market house built, according to Collinson, in 1616, on or near the site of the mediaeval market cross. It was still standing and functioning in 1750, with a large room over, used as a school room, but was converted to dwellings in about 1791. Later, much of the structure was demolished and a substantial red brick building constructed on the site, long occupied by Mr. C. C. Wallis, a surgeon. In 1853, to exploit the potential for trade occasioned by the advance of the railway network, the Market House Company was formed under the provisions of the Joint Stock Companies Act, with a capital of £2,500 in £25 shares, to construct and operate a new market house for the sale of corn, butter, cheese, meat, vegetables and other produce. F. C. Penrose was commissioned as architect, and the resulting structure was built at a cost of £2,300 and opened 2nd October 1855, with a dinner for 150, presided over by Theodore Thring. The building, distinctive in design, contained a variety of facilities on the two floors above the market area, as well as cells and custodian's quarters. There is no evidence that the pillars were re-used from an earlier structure, as is suggested in some accounts. The clock was erected in 1857 by subscription and restored in 1882. The anticipated financial rewards were never forthcoming, but the Market House Company survived until recent times, with the building fulfilling various functions if not the ones originally intended, including a long period as a cinema after the first cinematograph productions in 1903. The museum and tourist office now occupy the greater part of the building.

GEORGE HOTEL

The "George Hotel", one of Cary's most venerable structures, dates from the seventeeth century, if not earlier, and several stones clearly salvaged from the castle are visible in the external walls. There is a date stone for 1673 on the lane side of the building. Formerly a stone arched gateway led from the Market Place to the interior of the inn, on the key stone of which was carved a representation of St. George; during the eighteenth century the premises were re-fronted and the dragon, steed and hero taken down, and like the mediaeval cross which stood before it, used to repair the rutted street. A painted version was substituted, surmounted by intricate ironwork, aptly attributed in 1841 with "the gift it possesses of luring the benighted way-worn passenger by the monotonous creaking of its rusty hinges". The back portions were rebuilt after a destructive fire in 1845, caused by the ostler, Edward Biggin, entering the tallet with a candle.

One of the more prominent hostelries in the town; it was served by the "North Devon" coach, and subsequently became the parcel office for the G.W.R., serving at various times the function of post and excise office, it was also a well known venue for cock fighting and "sword and dagger". Prominent amongst its landlords were the Harrold family who presided from 1835–1904. F. E. Harrold and his son were noted auctioneers, and many local properties changed hands here during their occupation.

Little altered in appearance despite the removal of the rough-cast from the front elevation, the premises retain much of their historic charm and appeal particularly to the tourist trade.

The Liberal Parliamentary Candidate is here visiting the George Hotel, while his coachmen attend to his conveyance outside. Taken in the 1890s, the picture is a splendid evocation of the period.

The George Hotel in a view of about 1920. Motor transport was now superceding horse drawn traffic, hence the "garage" sign. The rough-cast wall finish was later removed.
(photo A. V. Pearse)

Facing the Market Place is the "Angel Inn", in a view from the 1890s. With origins in the eighteenth century, when it was known as "The Catherine Wheel" it prospered with the proximity of Cary markets. "Single-stick", a somewhat violent pastime, was last played before the Angel in about 1846, when the victor's prize was a new hat, and until 1835 a maypole, decorated with garlands of flowers and evergreens and surmounted by a flag was erected each year in the same location. It was also the custom to punish minor felonies by the practice of whipping at the cart's tail - the miscreants being dragged through the town from the "Angel" to the Park gates. The last woman so punished was in 1791, the last victim a man called Barber in the 1820s for stealing apples. Castle Cary was noted for the large number of public houses in relation to the size of the population, and the magistrates were anxious to reduce the number of such premises. The "Angel" survived longer than many, eventually closing in the late 1950s and the premises are now Chinn's antique shop.

The last night at the Angel Hotel, in about 1960. *Left to right, front:* Jack Talbot, seated; Tom Biss (Landlord); Mrs. Biss.
Middle row: Ken Clothier; Claude Kirkby; Mr. Higdon; Tom King; Bert Southway; Bert Bond; N.K.; George Stockley.
Back row: Mr. Francis; NK; Dudley Perrott; Bill Peaty.

Stuckeys Bank, seen here in 1909, has a front in a continental semi-baroque style that one would expect to find more in somewhere like Vienna than in Castle Cary. The building was reconstructed in 1891, when this front was built. As the inscription states, the firm was established in 1826, in Langport. Castle Cary had a branch soon afterwards, run by an agent; Thomas Mathews, of Florida Street, being the agent from 1835–40. Later, the agency moved to Bruton, and the resulting outcry led Theodore Thring to take up the campaign to restore the agency in 1852. Success came in 1856 and Stuckeys returned and opened on this site. In 1909, Stuckeys was replaced by a more powerful Company, Parr's Bank Ltd. The premises are now occupied by the National Westminster Bank. *(photo B. Lush)*

A view, which sadly has not survived in good condition, showing cattle in the High Street in about 1890. On market days both the Market Place and High Street were given over to the display and sale of livestock and other agricultural produce and implements, indeed this had been since mediaeval times the primary function of this area of the town. *(photo R. Biddiscombe)*

A view from 1903 of Florida House at the height of its splendour. Built in 1887 for John Stephens Donne, the rope, twine and webbing manufacturer, by E. O. Francis & Son, it was a flamboyant and ostentatious residence, complete with tower and belvedere. The architect was Charles Bell. Florida House was built on a green-field location to the west of the original Florida Place, on the site now occupied by the stable block of its successor, and which may incorporate some elements of its structure. This house was built by Robert Clarke, who was associated with Dennis Rolle, the promoter of an emigration scheme to Florida who visited Ansford in 1769 and planted a cotton shrub. The name Florida may derive from this connection, or perhaps from earlier owners, the Powell family, also possessors of a mansion at Florida Strata in Cardiganshire. Certainly the name was in use by 1803. Thomas Matthews purchased the property in 1828, including a silk house which he adapted for hair cloth production, this building being replaced by his son in 1865, and surviving on the east side of the complex. Florida House was utilised by the military during World War Two after which it was purchased by a Roman Catholic order, "The Convent of the Visitation". "The Sisters of Jesus Crucified" succeeded in 1959, and operated a guest house and printing business from the premises, known as "St John's Priory", before returning to France after 30 years. The property was then acquired by developers and has since seen the conversion of the ancillary buildings to residential use and construction of new houses in the grounds, sadly to the detriment of the original conception of the site. *(photo K. Wright)*

Cottages in the Upper High Street in about 1890, from a glass plate negative. Note that here, as is seen elsewhere in Castle Cary, the lower courses of the walls are built in blue lias stone rather than the Cary stone used for the remainder, presumably because the former is more resistant to crumbling as a result of rising damp. These cottages have been somewhat altered, with removal of the leaded window panes and replacement of the bay window.
(photo N. Foster)

A view of the upper High Street in 1900, showing the row of low thatched cottages adjoining Ochiltree House, which were demolished in August 1904, to be replaced by the building presently occupying this site fronting the nurseries.
(photo A. V. Pearse)

Residents of the Jubilee Cottages, five pairs of almshouses, built by John Boyd in 1887, take a break from work on their allotments in the early 1900s. *From left to right:* C/Sgt Hebditch; William Wyatt; Walt Chamberlain; Miss Coles; Mrs Burnett and Mrs J. Apsey. Hidden from view, in the middle distance, and running below ground level is Ansford Road, with, in the background to the right, Wesley House, the Methodist Manse, built in 1898 by C. Thomas & Sons at a cost of £1,100. The Jubilee Cottages, after a period of dereliction, were demolished in the 1980s and modern flats, known as Hanover Court, built on the site of the allotments. Wesley House was extended during the 1980s and now operates as a residential care home, known as Blackberry Hill.

Workmen are here engaged in boring a well behind Manor Farm at the foot of Lodge Hill in September 1908, prior to the construction of the pumping station by the Water Company in 1909. Frederick Winters is seen looking out of the bore hole, and Walter Eaton stands third from the right. He was an employee of Oliver Bartlett, an Ansford blacksmith. *(photo John Eaton)*

The northern and eastern parts of Castle Cary are shown in this view from 1973. In the centre, the Crendon building alongside John Boyds factory buildings is clearly visible as a recent addition to the Strode Components factory complex. Adjoining the site are the glasshouses of Wheadons Nursery. The Jubilee Cottages along Ansford Road are still standing, and Catherine's Close has yet to be developed. In the foreground there are several new houses next to the Methodist Chapel, and towards Ansford work has just started on housing development in Florida Fields, which was soon to expand into the Churchfields area.
(photo R. Hanley)

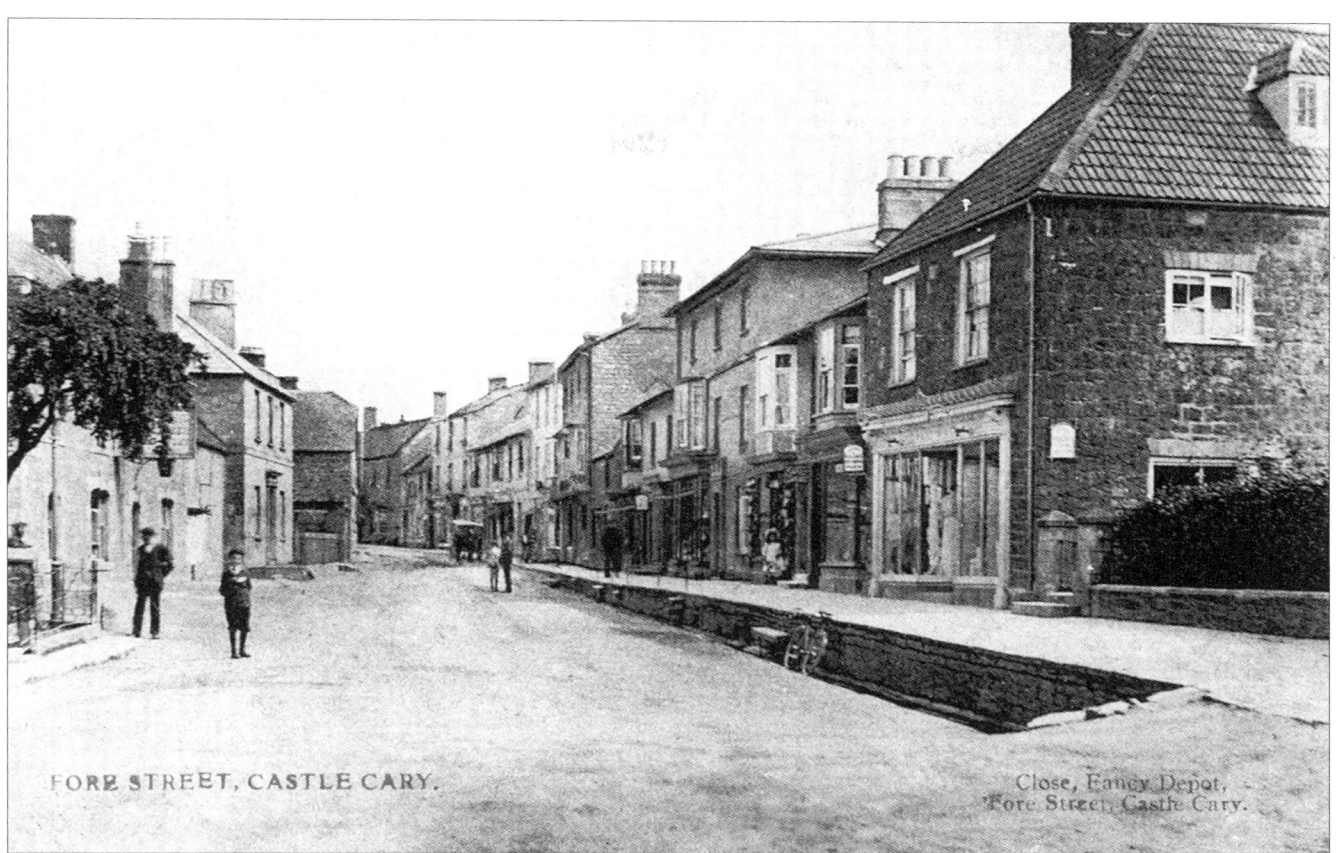

Fore Street from the south in 1909, showing the open stream running alongside the pavement. David Ash's draper's shop is in the foreground, right, the White Hart on the left. The barn jutting into the street beyond belonged to Barrett Bros. and was used as a stable, but demolished in the 1920s. *(photo A. V. Pearse)*

Fore Street, looking south, in September 1966. In the background the Fire Station has been erected, otherwise this view is little changed from earlier decades. *(photo A. V. Pearse)*

A view of Fore Street being excavated for the laying of electric cables in 1936 to supply mains electricity throughout the town. Ansford also had access to the supply. Electric power had been introduced to Castle Cary by Barrett Bros., in 1897, and usage had gradually increased, supplied by private lighting plants operated by stationary engines. Gas lighting, which had first appeared in Castle Cary in 1854, and for street lighting in 1859, continued in use for many years - indeed persisted until the 1970s. In the background is the White Hart, first opened in 1836, then substantially re-built and given a new front in 1872. On this site previously stood a house with a green in front, and open ditch bordering the street. *(photo B. Norton)*

Occupying the premises in Fore Street now the "Newstore" was the long established tailoring business of E. A. Churchouse, seen here during the late 1920s with a shop front installed in 1923. Many years earlier it was a private house, occupied by Mrs. Mary Coles, a dressmaker. This two-storey, three-bay building adjoined to the west a three-storey, three-bay block with a matching two-storey block on the far side, all built to the same design and with each block possessing a pair of doors in the centre surmounted by crenellations. All were erected about the middle years of the 19th century on the site of the yard of the Phoenix Inn which occupied the building subsequently Mr. Ash's drapery shop and later Otton's electrical store. Although insertion of a series of shop fronts has radically altered the appearance of the buildings, elements of the original design are still discernible. Note also the step over the stream which formerly ran along this side of the street and is now culverted.
(photo Mrs. D. Churchouse)

A view of Fore Street from about 1900 when it was arguably in its most attractive state. In the foreground to the right, is the Jubilee Fountain, erected by subscription in 1897 to commemorate Queen Victoria's Diamond Jubilee. Beneath is the stream running the length of Fore Street. The structure had a short life, being demolished in the early 1920s to clear the area for construction of the War Memorial in the Horse Pond. The fate of the pieces remains a mystery. Beneath the site is the Shoot, one of the sources of the River Cary.

AT THE FOUNTAIN

One evening, when the moon was bright,
My Jim and I, by her silvery light,
Took a walk on the Horsepond Esplanade,
When all of a sudden he stopped and said
"Let's look at the Jubilee Fountain."

So we paused and looked at that structure bold –
(Erected in '97 I'm told
As a memorial of our gracious Queen,
Who for sixty years on the throne had been) –
That wonderful Jubilee Fountain!

Says Jim, "I'm blowed if it aint a fraud;
It looks as tho' in two 'twere sawed,
And the 'tother side, where the spout is placed,
It seems to me the thing's three-faced!
This bally old Jubilee Fountain."

We listened in vain for the watery flow,
But it did not come – Oh, no! Oh, no!
Says Jim, "My dear, do you wonder why
When I come home I'm always dry,
When I can't get a drink at the Fountain?"

My Jim and I, disgusted quite,
(Perhaps 'twas wrong, perhap 'twas right),
Across the road we made our way,
Where beer flows quicker, so folks say,
Than water at the Fountain.

Betsy

Opposite page An aerial view of the Manor Farm complex, c1960, and its environs. Immediately to the east of this area (to the top of the photograph) are the buried remains of the castle keep, discovered and marked in 1890. Further information on the castle and its history can be obtained in "The Castles of Cary" by C. P. Hershon, and in articles in the Proceedings of the Somerset Archaeological and Natural History Society, especially Vol. XVI, 1890. The castle was succeeded, in due course, by a manor house, which seems to have been very large, and to have occupied, roughly, the same position as the present Manor Farm. Presumably the stone for this house was quarried out of the keep and other castle ruins. Thomas Gerard, in 1633, described it as "a house built by the Zouches within the verge of the castle walls", and the vestiges of this structure were mentioned by John Collinson in 1791: "The manor house stands on the east side of the street, and was, as appears by several fine old arches and other remains, a stately edifice, but great part of it has lately been demolished and the apartments which remain are converted into store rooms ... to the west of the house, and within twenty feet of the walls, was ... Park-Pond".

James Woodforde a few years before refers to a "court house" on this site being utilized for functions, suggesting that a substantial part of the house or its ancillary buildings was still standing.

It was almost certainly here that Charles II was sheltered on his flight from the battle of Worcester in 1652, as described in a contemporary manuscript: "The Lord Wilmot (as his Majesty's Harbinger) rode to Trent on Monday to make way for his more private reception there, and on Tuesday morning, September 16th, his Majesty's ague being then (as was pretended) in the recess, he repaired to the stable, and there gave orders for making ready the horses. And then it was signified from Mrs. Lane (though before so agreed) that William Jackson (the assumed name of the King) should ride single and carry the portmanteau. Accordingly they mounted, being attended part of the way by one of Mr. Norton's men as a guide, and that day rode through the body of Somersetshire to Mr. Edward Kirton's house at Castle Cary, near Bruton, where his Majesty lay that night, and next morning arrived at Colonel Wyndham's said house which was about twenty-six miles from Leigh".

Memory of the house's part in the King's successful flight did not save it from demolition, however. The farm buildings were constructed from its masonry, and numerous worked stones originating from the castle were identified by inspection in 1890, especially in the walls round the rick yard of the Manor House (the 19th century successor, which still stands).

Interpretation of the recent archaeological work will no-doubt clarify the successive developments on this site.

Other points of interest are that the Cary stocks stood on the site of the cottage by the Horse Pond and the entrance to Manor Farm. The land was purchased by Charles Moody and the stocks destroyed between 1830-40. Alongside the entrance-way to the farm is the Fire Engine House, built in 1856 on land given by Sir Henry Hoare. The primitive engine it housed was last used in about 1868 and sold in 1892. *(photo J. & D. Churchouse)*

Manor Farm buildings were demolished in 1999 to facilitate the construction of the development known as "Castle Rise". The rubble was passed through a stone crusher and recycled. Various archaeological investigations were undertaken, and significant, if complex, discoveries made. Manor Farm House is visible behind the excavator. *(photo J. & D. Churchouse)*

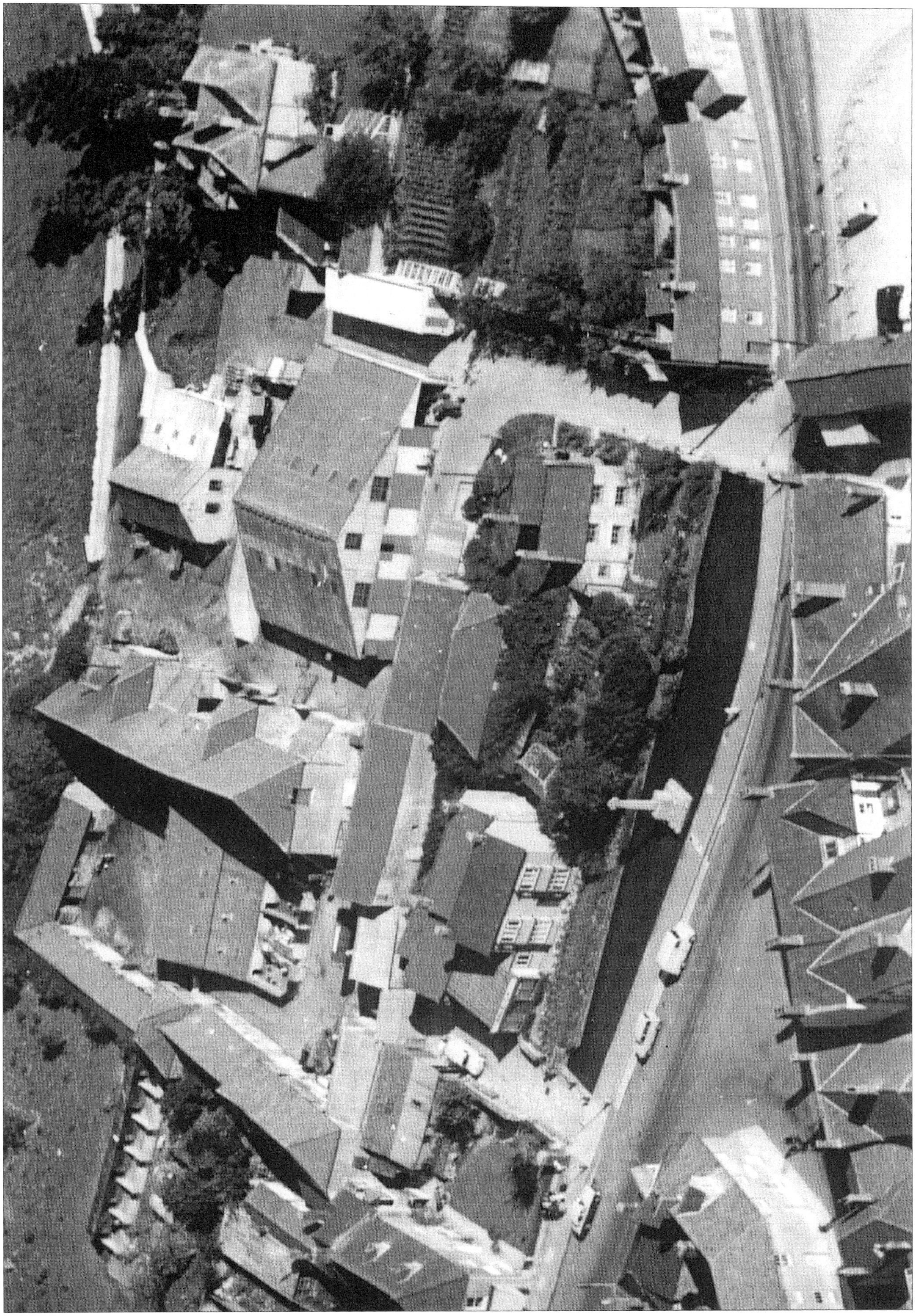

Now known as "The Horse Pond Inn", the "Britannia Inn" was opened about 1800, and several of the early landlords were of the Andrews family, whose naval connections perhaps led to the embodiment of the spirit of Trafalgar in the patriotic name and decoration. There were formerly various examples of this theme, including a large Union Jack painted on the ceiling and the inscription *'England expects that every man this day will do his duty'*. Above the roof the Union Jack was often hoisted, as is shown in early prints. A thriving Cary club, the "United Britons" was founded here in 1834, and the premises hosted the inaugural meeting of the Castle Cary Agricultural Society in 1852. Maritime links continued with the tragic loss of Samual Herman, a former landlord, in the Titanic disaster in 1912. The site has been discovered to be that of a former swamp, revealed by the digging of a well at a depth of 13 feet below the present ground level. The photograph dates from the 1890s. *(photo B. Lush)*

A view taken from the Church tower in the 1920s showing the Cary roofscape, with Mr. T. Lydford's veterinary buildings beyond the paddock in the foreground, and the Parsons Bros., wheelwrights shop behind them, now part of the Horse Pond Motel complex. The paddock and orchard have since been developed as the Fire Station, car park, toilets and Phillips garage. *(photo Mrs.L. Powell)*

HORSE POND

Tradition has long held that the Horse Pond was originally part of the castle moat and recent archaeological work on the site of the "Castle Rise" development has supported this view, and indicated that it was formerly somewhat larger in extent. From time immemorial it has belonged to the town and not to any private individual, and in 1784 was walled and paved. Early engravings show it looking much as it does at present. In 1885 an adjoining property owner attempted to fill the pond but the attempt was stopped and in the following year the pond was thoroughly cleaned out, repaired and its appearance improved by planting flowers and shrubs under the wall at the back.

Some of Wesley's early preachers were thrown into the Horse Pond and were far from being the only persons to be so treated.

Swans have long been associated with the pond, and it is only in recent years that attempts to maintain their presence have been abandoned. Since the nearby Park Pond was improved in 1846 swans were regularly introduced to either or both locations but tended to fall victim to accidents of various sorts. Unfortunately the Horse Pond is no longer considered of sufficient size to accommodate a pair of swans, and a sculptured substitute is now being considered. It can be noted that three swans appeared in the arms of the first Lords of Cary.

Black swans were introduced to the Horse Pond in July 1974 and are seen here settled into their new home. *(photo R. Pearce)*

A charming view taken of Church Villa of about 1905 revealing many aspects of its evolution from origins in the 17th century, indicated by the layout of the door and windows, the latter being Georgian framed sashes, which with the covering of the front elevation with stucco gave the house a more fashionable appearance. The Victorian period is represented by the ornate cast iron porch, the two monkey puzzle trees which stood on the lawn in front of the house and extensive plantings of laurel and box. Originally a part of the Hoare estate, the property, which included outbuildings and orchards where the Fire Station now stands, was purchased in 1899 by Barrett Bros. for £530. It is now known as "The Old Rectory" though there is no evidence that it fulfilled this function in recent centuries. *(photo A. V. Pearse)*

The old hollow oak tree on Lodge Hill, shortly before it was burnt down by vandals on 22nd July 1987. Behind is the Primary School showing the supplementary classrooms added to the original buildings.

This Turnpike cottage stood at the end of Broadway Lane on the B3152 between Abbey and Smallway and was built during the establishment of the turnpike system in the 18th century, and demolished in the 1960s when it was owned by Henry S. Perrott. *(photo R. Perrott)*

A view of the sandbanks' at the junction of South Street and Church Street in 1905. The ground level behind the trees is the natural surface, indicating how the passage of traffic along the road combined with erosion by water has over many centuries cut through the soft sandy bedrock. The earliest settlement was probably in this area near the church and the long narrow tenement plots on either side of South Street extending from this point are possibly the result of a settlement pattern established by the overlord of the castle in the early Norman period. The large four storey building in the background has been demolished since the photograph captured this scene. *(photo A. V. Pearse)*

A view along South Street, looking north, taken in 1906. In the foreground, to the left, is Annandale, so named by John "Packer" Hill, after his native area of Dumfriesshire. He was one of several Scotch drapers who came to Castle Cary in the late 19th century to establish their enterprises. John Hill had arrived in 1881, aged 20, and entered the drapery and outfitting business carried on by Mr. Mitchell in South Cary, before commencing business on his own. He married Mary Carlyle Stewart, great niece of the famous Victorian writer Thomas Carlyle, and on the pavement are two of their children, Margaret and David, together with the manservant and maid. In the middle distance, again on the left, is the cheese store belonging to another Scotsman, James Mackie, a cheese factor, who operated a well-known business from the town. *(photo A. V. Pearse)*

South Cary House is an imposing and substantial residence fronting South Street, now utilized as a residential home. During the 18th century it was the residence of "Justice" Creed, the local magistrate, who on occasion faced a menacing mob outside. Calmer times came with his successor, Rev. Francis Woodforde, followed by the Gray family in the 1830s and 40s. Later it became a girls' school run by Misses Amelia and Marianne Beak, until about 1884. More recent owners, who carried out considerable modifications, were T. S. Donne and F. G. Lemon. Except for the presence of the chimney, the view of 1910 shows the house very much as it remains today. *(photo A. V. Pearse)*

"Salisbury Terrace", overlooking Station Road at the junction of Torbay Road, was a block of houses commissioned in a pleasing contemporary style with elements of the arts and crafts movement, by Castle Cary Parish Council and built in 1913, together with a similar block, seen here in the background, known as "Moore Villas". The photograph shows them soon after construction. A more ambitious but architectually much more austere housing development was undertaken by the local authority further along Station Road, between the wars, known as West Park. *(photo B. Lush)*

A view of Torbay from the railway bridge in 1903 is an essentially pastoral scene of small fields containing hay ricks. The road was formerly known as Mill Lane and it was here, along the course of the River Cary, that industrial development took place, utilizing water power, in the early 19th century. Light industrial and service businesses have continued this tradition, and the area has been developed almost as far as the crossroads, long known as Fulford's Cross. The mill building used as a dairy factory in the middle distance has been demolished, but subsequent development has included R. Allen's concrete works, Centaur Services, and most recently the Delaware Veterinary practice. *(photo A. V. Pearse)*

Opposite the Torbay Road junction with Station Road and to some extent hidden from view are a block of cottages built in 1892 as four almshouses known as Poor House Steps. They are now called Four House Steps, and Nos. 1 to 3 have been combined leaving No. 4 as an individual residence. The gothic design of the windows adds character, and is similar to that seen at the former Hillcrest School, and on the former Turnpike cottage near the railway station. *(photo Mrs K. Cross)*

A view of the Constitutional Club and adjoining areas in 1975. The tennis courts were sold for housing development in the 1980s, as was the disused Donnes allotment field behind them. In the foreground are Salisbury Terrace and the former almshouses at a right angle to Station Road. *(photo B. Lush)*

The Constitutional Club in Station Road, shown here in 1913, was opened on 28th September 1911 by Herbert Pike-Pease, M.P. for Darlington. It was built on land donated by T. Salisbury Donne by H. W. Pollard and Son of Bridgwater for £1,500 and replaced premises in Woodcock Street, opened in 1896 by Earl Selborne, which then became the Liberal Club. The new building contained dwelling quarters, a hall and a skittle alley, and continues to thrive, having been adapted and extended as required. The area of tennis courts adjoining was sold for housing development in the 1980s.
(photo A. V. Pearse)

A view of the rear of the building on the day of opening in 1911. *(photo A. V. Pearse)*

Above Park Lodge, recently built, from a glass plate of 1890. *(photo N. Foster)*
Below Park Lodge in 1980, mellowed by nearly a century, but little altered with the porch and ground floor window modification both in the spirit of the original design. *(photo N. Foster)*

Above The "Central Garage" in Fore Street, with proprietor Jack Norris in his taxi cab in 1938. *(photo M. Dunn)*.
Below With a new front as Dave Marsh's Hardware Store in 1999. *(photo D. Marsh)*

Above Squibb's Garage in 1986, shortly before demolition. It was itself the development of the site of the Victorian brickworks.
(photo R. Pearce)
Below The high density and rather utilitarian development on the site of Squibb's Garage in 1987, known as Victoria Court.
(photo R. Pearce)

Jack Pike's house built in 1936 and former cycle shop between Manor Farm and the Horse Pond in 1997, shortly before demolition. *(photo Mrs. V. Nicholls)*

A row of houses, complete ultimately with false chimneys, undergoing construction behind the Horse Pond in 2000, as part of the "Castle Rise" development. *(photo R. Boyer)*

A view of park Pond and Castle Cary Church from Lodge Hill c1910. An example of a quality chromolithgraphic postcard produced by Wilkinson and Co of Trowbridge. *(photo A. V. Pearse)*

Castle Cary's best preserved Victorian shop front is that of T. White and Sons, Ironmongers and Implement Dealers. The shop is a veritable Aladdin's cave of treasures and contains a wonderfully ornate cast iron spiral staircase. Thomas White established his business here in 1883. The premises were rebuilt by Anthony Nancolas in 1804, his initials with those of his wife are incorporated in the façade. *(photo Mrs V. Nicholls)*

Castle Cary

Dating from 1906 is this view from Lodge Hill of Park Pond with the Council Schools and parish church in the background. A beautiful example of quality chromolithographic printing of the period. It was printed in Saxony for Wilkinsons of Trowbridge and epitomises the artistic qualities achieved by some early postcards. Park Pond derives from a series of springs issuing from Lodge Hill, and principally from one called Lady's Spring, a dedication to the Virgin Mary, and is the source of the River Cary. It is probably also a relic of the castle moat. In its present state it was created from "a wide morass, covered with spear reeds, that previously disgraced the town", by Charles Moody in 1846 and after improvement was a pretty sight, with an island, fishing boats, swans and flowers and even on occasion able to bear skaters - in 1855 it was frozen for six weeks and again in 1890/1 when it was decorated with Chinese lanterns. Sadly, in more recent times its condition has deteriorated. *(photo A. V. Pearse)*

The Vicarage, Castle Cary

Castle Cary Vicarage, seen here in 1910, was built in 1846 by Canon Richard John Meade, Vicar 1845–1880, at his sole expense, on a "greenfield site" though it is likely that a route, of which South Street and Victoria Road are remaining sections, originally crossed the area, bordered by the Saxon and early Norman settlement. Prior to its construction, Cary had not possessed a Vicarage for at least 150 years, as the living was held with that of Ansford where the parson resided. The Vicarage was built on a scale commensurate with the position enjoyed by wealthy members of the Victorian clergy and was very much a "gentleman's residence" accommodating an appropriate level of staff. Premises of this size became an ever increasing burden during the 20th century and a new, smaller Vicarage was constructed in 1974. This house was subsequently sold. Many events were held in the grounds, notably the "Pastoral Plays" in the decade before the First World War. *(photo A. V. Pearse)*

WEATHER

An electrical storm over Castle Cary in 1991 provides this striking photograph taken from Knights Yard. *(photo B. Lush)*

The winter of 1962/63 was the hardest since 1947 with many minor roads completely blocked with snowdrifts for over three weeks. Milk had still to be collected from farms and as it was transported in churns it could be hauled across fields to reach open roads, if necessary. Shown here is a lorry load of milk churns stuck in the snow at Turnpike Cottage between Castle Cary and Galhampton. *(photo P. Brewin)*

In 1967 Wakes Coaches double decker was marooned in snowdrifts at Abbey Cottages on the B3152. *(photo R. Perrott)*

Snowdrifts in the road at the entrance to Sportman's Lodge in 1978. *(photo J. Rose)*

Fore Street blocked with snow in 1978, the last occasion when this occurred. *(photo J. Rose)*

The River Brue in flood in 1982 between the station and the road to Sutton behind Moff Motors. *(photo D. George)*

AGRICULTURE

The parishes of Castle Cary and Ansford, comprising 2,625 and 844 acres respectively, are situated on fertile lias soils; the more elevated areas having light sandy soils derived from "inferior oolite", with heavier clays in the lower parts. Today the landscape is almost entirely pasture, though this is a comparatively recent development. In the mediaeval period an open landscape of arable cultivation predominated - aerial photographs reveal the traces of ridge and furrow cultivation - with mainly a wheat, beans, fallow, rotation, although some other crops were grown. Both Ansford and Castle Cary had deer parks, which were left to pasture and woodland, as were the steeper slopes, while wetter areas provided meadow herbage.

Thomas Gerard reported in 1633 "two parkes whereof the one remaines unto this daye stored with deere; the other, being a mile off at Almsford, as all the rest of demeasnes, leased out ... below this towne and belonging to it lyes a large flatt or rich ground called Carymoore of late inclosed ..."

The evolution of the present landscape had begun, but it was a slow process. John Billingsley observed in 1795, "I cannot pass over this neighbourhood without noticing the pleasant and fertile parish of Castle Cary, which, both in respect to soil and climate, cannot well be excelled ... In Castle Cary potatoes are grown on a very large scale, and it is no unusual thing to get one hundred and sixty sacks (two hundred and fifty pounds each) per acre, the average price about five shillings per sack." Even in 1836 Wm. Phelps was able to say that the "soil in the higher part of the parish is a fine sandy loam almost exclusively appropriated to the growth of potatoes." Flax was also widely grown to supply the local textile industry but by the early 19th century was in decline and died out in 1860.

The piecemeal process of enclosure had been completed by this time and with it came the pattern of small and middle-sized farmsteads with their substantial buildings, which survived until recent years. Pasture, supporting a growing dairy industry, became the norm, though mixed farming was still the rule well into the 20th century. Cider orchards had also expanded in the early 19th century, and once planted tended to persist. The coming of the railway assisted marketing of produce; dairy production remained profitable in the agricultural depression of the late 1800s, and Prideaux's built a creamery at the station in 1910, while a mill was converted to a butter factory at Torbay.

Castle Cary was a thriving agricultural centre - Castle Cary Agricultural Society was formed in 1852 and ran a series of Shows, and in 1889 amalgamated with the Bruton and Wincanton Societies. Agricultural machinery and requisites were retailed by T. White and others over a wide area, and the appropriately named Caleb Loader of Ansford invented a harvester for loading crops of hay and corn.

Two World Wars, the depression of the 1930s, and mechanization were, however, to have a major impact on local agriculture. The number of farms has rapidly declined over recent decades, and very few small farms survive. Fields have of necessity been made larger, and machinery has replaced much of the workforce. Silage has replaced hay, and grass leys much permanent pasture, and in recent years maize has become a popular crop. Cider orchards have almost disappeared and many old barns have been converted for housing. These changes are but one of the many agricultural transformations that the area has witnesssed.

THURSDAY, February 21st, 1907.

CASTLE CARY.

7th ANNUAL

SHOW AND SALE

OF

Pedigree and Pure Bred Shorthorn, Devon, Hereford, or any other breed

BULLS.

WHEN UPWARDS OF

30 GUINEAS IN OPEN PRIZES

AND SILVER CHAMPION CUP.

will be given by gentlemen of the neighbourhood and the Auctioneers for Bulls bona-fide sold by Auction.

☞ In case of Prize Winners being bought in, the Prize won will be forfeited and handed on, according to the order of merit awarded by Judges, down to highly commended honours, with the exception of the Cup, which will only be awarded to the Champion or Reserve Champion Bull.

☞ On no account will an entry for Show be accepted after February 7th.

MOODY & SON,   **C. M. MOODY,**
Auctioneers,   Secretary,
EVERCREECH, Somerset.   EVERCREECH, Somerset.

J. H. Roberts, Printer, Castle Cary.

Castle Cary Bull Show was first held on 12th March 1901, with 55 animals, in the Auction Field at Millbrook and thereafter became a well patronized annual event, popular with farmers from a wide area. The view dates from 1906, with bowler hats appearing to be the most popular headgear for farmers at this time; and the show programme from 1907.
(photo B. Lush) (programme A. V. Pearse)

54

A view of Lower Cockhill Farm from the west, taken in 1913. Long in the possession of the Hoare family of Stourhead, it was occupied for much of the 19th century by the Allen family, who left in 1919, when it was sold by the estate to W. J. Barrett. He moved to Ansford in 1922 and the farm was later purchased by the Boyer family. To the right is the older portion of the house, now a separate dwelling. A fascinating survival, it dates from about 1400 and is a mediaeval hall house, with a two-bay hall, retaining much of the original woodwork in the roof, including a fine arch braced truss and wind-braces. Even more astonishing is the first floor jettied room over the front door. Approximately 10 feet square, and built of timber, wattle and daub, it was added in about 1500. During the 1970s and 1980s original and intricate wall paintings were discovered which have since been carefully preserved. There are also tiny squints giving a view in each direction along the road in the north and south walls. The main part of the farmhouse dates from the 17th century, from which time the remaining portion of the original house was down-graded to ancillary purposes. *(photo A. V. Pearse)*

Cider apples are here being hauled in a double horse Somerset wagon for unloading into the cider loft at W. J. Barrett's Lower Ansford farm on 22 October 1936. Cider was made using an electrically-operated hydraulic press and stored in casks. Bottled cider was also produced. One of a series of photographs, several of which appeared in *The Times* of 24th October 1936. *(photo A. V. Pearse)*

Rick building at Lower Ansford in about 1950 utilizing an elevator powered by a stationary engine; within a very few years the ancient art of rick building was to disappear as baled hay became the norm, and with it the skill of rick thatching and the need for thatching spars obtained from the pollard willows which were grown around many field ponds. Sarah Barrett is wielding the pitchfork.
(photo A. V. Pearse)

The first set of triplets born from artificial insemination by Horlicks AI Centre based at Higher Flax Mills at Castle Cary, in September 1950 to *Shayne*, the pet cow of Reg and Annie Lush, the well-known Cary butchers. The cow was named after an American soldier stationed in the town during the war, who became a friend of the Lush family.

An aerial view of Manor Farm with Park Pond in the foreground. Manor Farm, following the retirement of the Corp brothers, was purchased by Mr W. H. Longman in 1940, consisting of 168 acres, for £6,700. An additional 32 acres at Torbay was purchased for £2,650. The farmhouse and buildings are of largely 19th century date, constructed on the site of and from the materials of the extensive earlier manor house described by Collinson in the late eighteenth century, and itself built using materials from the castle keep which stood on the mound to the right of the site. The farm buildings were demolished in 1999 and the area was developed as a residential estate. *(photo J. & D. Churchouse)*

Mrs. Betty Churchouse with her young family and Harry the pony at Manor Farm in 1955. *(photo J. Churchouse)*

A view from Lodge Hill across Castle Cary, with Ditcheat Hill and the Mendips in the background, showing pig rearing during the 1960s. In the middle distance the earthworks of the outer bailey of the castle are clearly visible. *(photo Mrs Churchouse)*

Blessing of the plough ceremony on Plough Sunday at Manor Farm in the 1970s. *Left to right:* Guy Churchouse; Rev. Frank Hall (Vicar of All Saints); Bill Tallon; Peter Wyatt; Ken Targett and Ted Marsh. *(photo D. Churchouse)*

Mr. Bill Weeks operating a semi-automatic churn-washer at Manor Farm in 1950. Milk was transported in ten gallon churns which had superseded the conical seventeen gallon version used earlier in the century. Manor Farm was a well-known cheese-making establishment, winning the Champion Cheese prize at the Bath and West Show in 1974. *(photo Mrs Churchouse)*

State-of-the-art technology in operation at Cockhill in 1974 with grass drying by the Alvan Blanch Mark 3, capable of producing 300 tons of dried grass per season. Cheap fuel costs of 6p per gallon of diesel when this machine was installed in 1973 increased after the fuel crisis of the mid-1970s to over £1 per gallon in 1982 making this process uneconomical, and the equipment redundant. The tractor is one of the first Zetors to be imported to the UK in 1968, and has since been restored to its original condition. *(photo R. Boyer)*

From time immemorial livestock had been marketed in Castle Cary either in the Market Place, on Bailey Hill, or on a site later occupied by the nurseries in the High Street. The coming of "progress" and regulations meant that these sites were not deemed appropriate, and in 1911 the Board of Agriculture ordered the removal of Castle Cary market to an approved location, and the auction sale field, known as the "Britannia Paddock" was selected. Work on building the new market was undertaken in 1912 and it opened on 18th March 1913. The aerial photograph of 1960 shows the market site, top right, with the sale ring roofed in galvanized sheeting. The last sale to be held here was the Fortieth Castle Cary Bull Show and Sale, on 12th March 1940. No further sales were held and the Ministry of Agriculture withdrew the market licence in 1949. In the foreground, from the left, are the Triangle Stores, a newsagents, formerly fronting Poole's mineral water manufactory, seen behind, and in earlier times a corn mill. The Britannia Inn became the Horse Pond Inn in 1990. Dunster House and the public conveniences are on the right.
(photo R. Boyer)

E. LITMAN & SON,
BASKET & CHAIR MAKERS,
CASTLE CARY.

Now is the time to order Potato and Apple Baskets, Vegetable Hampers, Cross Handles.

How to obtain Eggs in Plenty all the coming Winter.—Apply as above. Information gratis.

Thomas White & Sons,

CASTLE CARY, Somerset.

GENERAL & FURNISHING IRONMONGERS

AND

IMPLEMENT DEALERS.

Intensive poultry rearing arks at Sportsmans Lodge Farm in the 1960s. The birds were reared for egg reproduction with each ark containing about 100 fowls and moved onto fresh grass daily.

T. White and Sons were noted retailers of agricultural machinery in Castle Cary and the surrounding area. They were main agents for Bamford and Nicholson. For many years the lower part of the Market House and area in front was used to store and display their stock as seen here in the 1930s. *(photo B. Lush)*

Triplets were born to an Ayrshire cow *Sportsmans Desiree* at Sportsmans Lodge Farm in 1979 and are seen here with thirteen-year-old Juliet White. The cow was champion at the Bath and West Show the previous year.

The barn at Grove Farm is the finest example of its type in Castle Cary parish, and was probably built in the early nineteenth century, but the design, with the central opposing waggon entrances, is based on the great monastic barns of the middle ages, commonly known as tithe barns. This example, which is no longer used for agricultural purposes, was sold for residential conversion in April 2002.

INDUSTRIES

Castle Cary's textile industries had their beginnings in the late eighteenth century with the arrival of entrepreneurs and new processes. The town was noted for the production of dowlais, tick and knit-hose, but during the previous centuries the wool trade had been dominant - indeed William Langland in his "Vision of Piers Plowman" of 1362 mentioned "cari-maury", a coarse quality woollen cloth, popular amongst pastoral workers, and there is evidence of foreign cloth workers settling in the 1570s.

However, the wool industry had long since declined, and its position was to some extent taken by the processing of flax. An Act of Parliament of 1781 encouraged flax growing and it was widely cultivated around Castle Cary into the early 19th century, the last crops being in the Mill Lane area about 1860. The River Cary provided motive power for several flax mills, as well as those processing flour and corn, and had the potential to power new enterprises, which was soon exploited.

The leather trade was also important, with a building called the Skin House near the Horse Pond for inspection of hides. Surprisingly, there was even an iron foundry in "Golden Lion" Yard, later Chapel Yard, in South Cary.

The revival began with the arrival of Charles Donne at Ansford in 1797 to manufacture twine, rope and sailcloth. He soon moved to Castle Cary. By 1822, 167 of the 333 families resident in Castle Cary were involved in trade or manufacture. Further opportunities were provided by the activities of Thomas Matthews, a girth-webb manufacturer of Yetminster, who moved his operations to Castle Cary, making girth-webbs and twine, opposite Chapel Yard in South Cary in 1815. By 1819 he owned 12 houses and land in Castle Cary and was the first to introduce horse-hair seating weaving to the town, building workshops in South Cary. In 1828 he purchased the Florida property from Robert Clarke, where there was evidently a silk factory, presumably built to exploit a limited opportunity arising from the decline of woollen and linen manufacture. The premises were converted to girth-webb and hair seating weaving, and he continued to increase his holdings, acquiring factory buildings on Bailey Hill, and further establishments at Milton Clevedon and Evercreech. Thomas Matthews died in 1863, but his son Thomas took over his businesses and built a new factory at Florida in 1865. The range of products using horse hair was expanding, and opportunities were not neglected. In 1837 John Boyd arrived, and was later to become Castle Cary's most prominent horse hair manufacturer.

The 20th century, like the 19th, has seen the decline and disappearance of many of Castle Cary's staple industries, but the town has adapted to changing circumstances. Manufacturing has involved shoe component making, and a concrete products works. Notable has been the increase in importance of service industries - the growth of the veterinary supply company Centaur Services being a prime example.

T. S. DONNE & SONS

By the late eighteenth century Cary's long established textile industry - the manufacture of dowlais, tick and knithose - was in decline, when Charles Donne, a manufacturer of twine, sail cloth and girth-webbing, born at Drayton in 1768, arrived from Langport in 1797 with six looms to commence business in cottages at Ansford, exploiting the supply of flax grown in the vicinity and the plentiful labour supply. He moved to Castle Cary in 1809, and by 1818 his business had prospered sufficiently to enable expansion from his premises in the town, to additional workshops at Torbay, comprising sailcloth shops and rope walks, with sheds nearby at Fulfords Cross for dyeing. Various members of the family operated the branches of the industry; Charles' son Charles Donne running the sail cloth works based at Woodville House and Woodcock Street, and son Thomas Salisbury Donne the premises in Mill Street.

Charles Donne (Senior) died in 1855, and Thomas Salisbury Donne formed the company of T. S. Donne & Sons shortly afterwards. He died in 1862. Charles Donne's Torbay Mills had been let to Albin Close, a flax spinner, but reverted to the Donnes after his death in 1863. They proved inadequate to house the expanding business, and were augmented by Thomas Salisbury Donne (Junior) in 1870 with the impressively substantial three storey, eleven bay structure with an octagonal chimney at Higher Flax Mills which survives largely intact to this day.

Powered initially by a water wheel utilizing the supply of water from the springs rising nearby to form the River Cary, the factory possessed a steam engine by 1848 and was converted to steam power in the 1860s, which continued to be used until installation of electric motors in the 1950s.

Twines, ropes and cordage, with webbing, were the firm's core products, and found a ready market in the upholstery trade. Wartime increased demand for many of their products, and new lines, such as camouflage nets and mosquito nets were readily exploited. The business, which had become a Limited Company in 1926, celebrated its 150th anniversary in 1947, but a decline in demand for its output followed and it merged with John Boyd Textiles Ltd., finally closing in the early 1980s.

The Donne family were prominent in local affairs and enthusiastic promotors of various enterprises in the town. Apart from the factory buildings at Higher Flax Mills, Florida House, built by John Stephens Donne in 1887, and South Cary Lodge, largely reconstructed by his nephew William Stephens Donne, remain as memorials to their prosperity.

A view of Higher Flax Mills from 1903, showing the rope walk in the foreground, with the steam powered mill building, built in 1870, behind. *(photo Mr. R. Collings)*

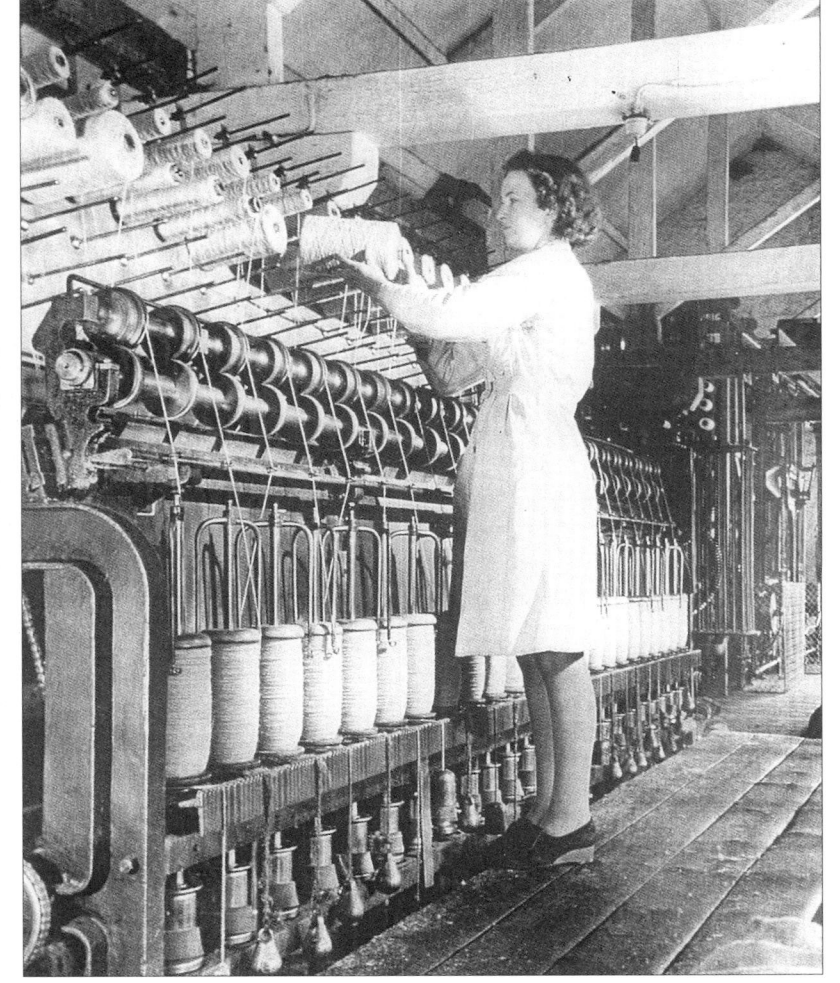

The ropewalk was eventually covered, and is here shown in 1948 housing machinery for weaving upholstery webbing for the furniture trade. During the Second World War the building had been requisitioned by the Ministry of Food for storing foodstuffs and painted externally in camouflage colours. It was returned to Donnes in 1947.
(photo Mr. D. Stickland)

Rope making c1950 - Florence Ridout winding the rope spools.
(photo Mr. D. Stickland)

The twine polishing machine, made by W. Bywater of Leeds, in use in 1948. *(photo Mr. D. Stickland)*

JOHN BOYD & CO. LTD.

A travelling draper, John Boyd, arrived in Castle Cary in 1837. Born in Ayrshire in 1815, he had migrated to Wincanton where he operated for several years before leasing a cottage in Chapel Yard, South Cary, and installing looms for the weaving of horse hair. By 1851 he was employing 30 women, 34 children and 9 men and needed to expand, and purchased the house he named Ochiltree House, with a narrow strip of land behind, in the Upper High Street, formerly the site of the sheep market.

Reached via a passageway through the house, he constructed what later became known as the "Ansford Factory" in 1851 - a three storey twelve bay building with ancillary blocks adjoining. Washing of the horse hair had still to be carried out at Torbay Road. In 1863 he acquired the adjoining property to the west - "The Villa" later "Beechfield House" with extensive areas of land alongside his original plot, enabling the expansion of his factory premises, as well as providing sites where he built Cumnock Terrace for some of his management and staff, and his philanthropic contribution, the Jubilee Cottages in 1887.

The Factory Acts and Education Act of 1870 restricted the use of child labour, previously an important element in the operation of hand looms. To replace the function of child "pickers" John Boyd commissioned Joseph Chapman and two assistants to invent a mechanical "picker" - successfully achieved in 1871 and patented in 1872; the resulting machines still being in use today. A new eleven bay building with serrated roof angled for natural lighting, was constructed to house the new power looms.

The enterprise was converted to a Limited Company in 1883, and John Boyd died in 1890. His company accountant and secretary, William Macmillan, whose father had been a friend of the Boyds in Ayrshire, took over the running of the business, which prospered, supplying various horse hair seating fabrics, furniture, stuffing, tailoring interlining fabrics and stiffeners, with up to 120 looms in operation.

The First World War served to increase demand for some horse hair products, but the boom was short-lived. The Russian revolution cut off a major source of supply of quality horse hair, while the supply in Britain dwindled with that of the number of horses. Markets for the finished products declined as changes in furniture design and stuffing prevailed and requirements for tailoring usage was reduced, to an extent that by the mid 1930s the horse hair industry had all but collapsed. The "Ansford Factory" never recovered from disruption caused when the Government commandeered much of the factory floorspace and only 40 looms were working in the early 1950s on a part time basis. The directors decided that retrenchment was the only option and the "Ansford Factory" and Ochiltree House were sold to Avalon Leatherboard Co., part of the C. & J. Clark Group, in 1956.

John Boyd and Co., moved to one of Donne's buildings at Higher Flax Mills in Torbay Road. Donnes had survived the Second World War in better shape, but their traditional products found it increasingly difficult to find a market. The firms merged in the mid 1970s as T. S. Donne and John Boyd and Co., but manufacture of twine and webbing ceased in the 1980s and Donne's machinery was scrapped. Horse hair fabrics began to experience a revival, for the covering of quality furniture and several prestigious orders saved what was now the only surviving horse hair fabric manufacturer in Britain. With a world-wide market for a specialist product, its future seems assured.

Boyds power looms are seen here producing woven hair-seating in about 1905, when the machinery had been in operation nearly thirty years. Chiefly Siberian horse hair was utilized and many thousands of yards of fabric were made every month. The looms were powered by means of belts from the overhead shafting, itself turned by steam power. A small number of hand-looms were still in operation at this time.
(photo Castle Cary Visitor)

Ochiltree House was so named by John Boyd, who purchased the property in 1851, after his native home in Ayrshire. The house dated from the early 1820s and was built by William Paine, a carpenter, on the site of some old cottages. A number of owners followed and the house was used as a school for a time. In 1845 it was occupied by Rev. R. Meade while Castle Cary Vicarage was being built. Ochiltree House is a five bay building built of Cary stone with the brick front fashionable at the time, as seen elsewhere in the town. The inscriptions over the cart passage reads "John Boyd and Co., Limited., Est 1837" and refers to the foundation of his business in Castle Cary, not to his removal to this site. Here he lived until his death in 1890, after which it was occupied by William Macmillan until 1911 and then by other members of the latter's family. Eventually converted into flats, the house deteriorated, until it was completely restored in 1979/80 by Strode Components and used as office accommodation and showrooms. *(photo C. & J Clark Ltd.)*

Boyd's Hair Factory building, constructed in 1851, is a most attractive and substantial addition to Castle Cary's industrial heritage. The twelve bay construction is of Cary stone on a Keinton lias plinth and is reminiscent of barrack blocks seen in Scottish towns, as well as possessing an air of permanence deriving from the confidence of the period. The architect is not known. The buildings added to the right were offices.
(photo C. & J. Clark Ltd.)

One of the Boyd "picker" looms dating from 1870 and invented by J. Chapman and W. Henderson still in use at John Boyd Textiles Ltd., at Higher Flax Mills in 1997. The design has never been improved upon.

AVALON LEATHERBOARD CO.

Avalon Leatherboard Co., was part of the C. & J. Clark Group founded at Street, and concerned with the production of leatherboard and related shoe components. Based originally in Street, the Company's need for additional manufacturing capacity resulted in the lease of a three storey building from Donnes in 1956 at Higher Flax Mills, which was then converted to a components factory employing 26 operatives, making insoles and insole strips. These premises were far from ideal so in 1960 Avalon Leatherboard purchased the vacant "Ansford Factory" from John Boyd and Co., for £8,000 and spent a further £12,000 converting it for the manufacture of insoles. The Higher Flax Mills building was abandoned in 1962, though the covered rope walk nearby was rented for the production of stiffeners and resin soles.

Production at the Ansford Factory was expanding, so a large new factory known as the Crendon Building was added in 1971/2, enabling the operation to employ over 200 in a variety of functions. In 1981 a last making plant was installed here. Production continued, the firm having become known as Avalon Components. Ochiltree House was restored in 1979 and utilised to house offices and showrooms for the complex.

During the 1980s the footwear trade in Britain had to adapt to the penetration of cheap foreign imports, and consequently Clarks increasingly turned to production of its output abroad. Manufacture of components in the U.K. became uneconomic and with the exception of the last making plant, which was transferred to Street, all production at the Ansford Factory and Higher Flax Mills rope walk building, ceased in 1992.

A view looking south between J. Boyd's North Light building and the Crendon building, taken in 1992. The dust extraction apparatus is visible on the side of the Crendon building, behind is the shed housing the emergency generator. *(photo J. Cocks)*

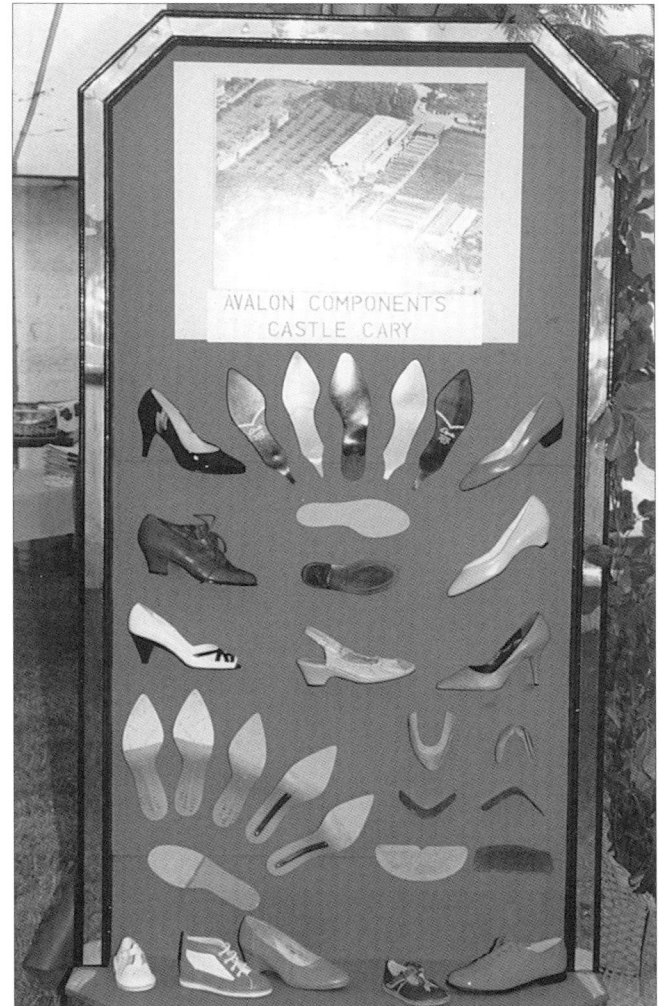

Left to right: Trevor Vincent; Nadine Powell and Janette Piroddu bevelling insoles in the North Light building at the Ansford Factory in 1990. *(photo J. Cocks)*

A display of resin soles, insoles and stiffeners, manufactured at Avalon Components, together with examples of shoes in which they were utilized. *(photo Avalon Components)*

John Cocks (Factory Engineer) with reserve pallets of plastic last blocks in the background, at the Ansford Factory in 1988. *(photo J. Nicholls)*

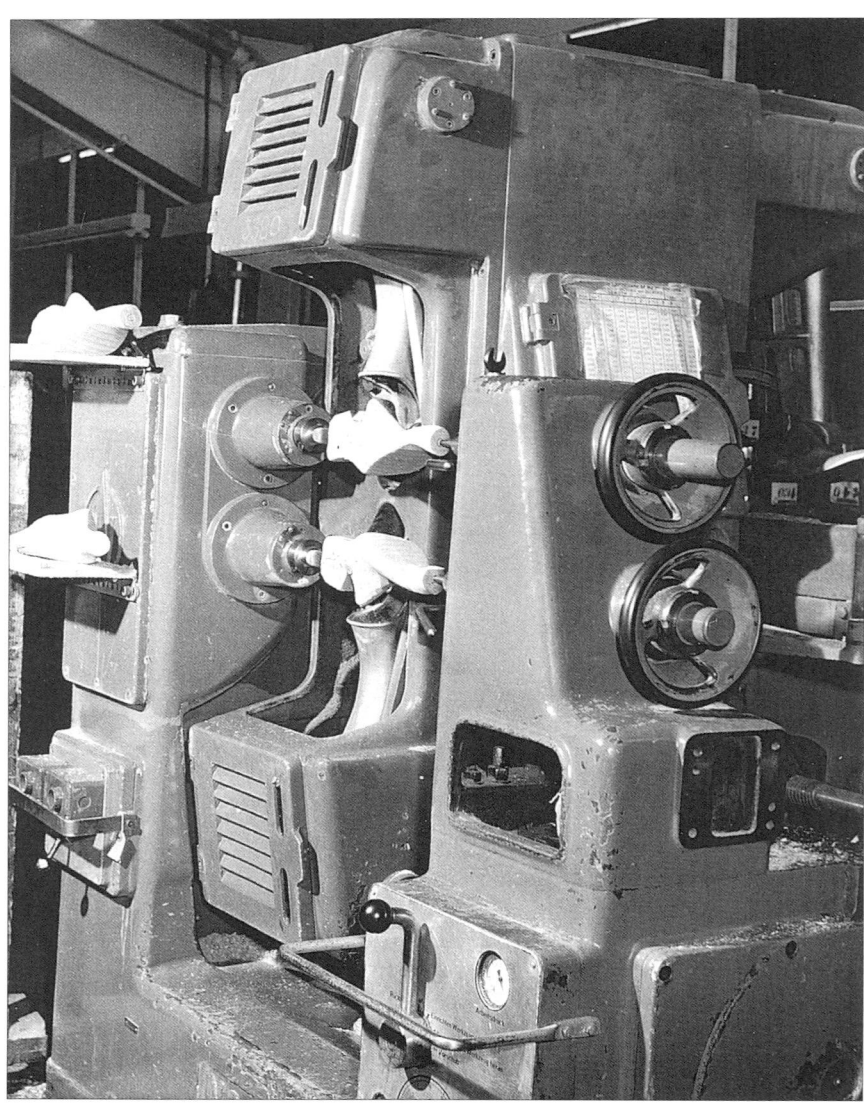

A pair of lasts being turned on an Incoma Copying Lathe in the Crendon building in 1984. *(photo C. & J. Clark Ltd.)*

CLANVILLE SAWMILLS

Clanville sawmills were established during the late 1870s by Jonathan Cruse, a native of Kintbury, Berks, dealing exclusively with home grown timber, especially the oak and elm so prevalent in the area. Timber was purchased from woods and fields, felled, and hauled to the sawmill yards for conversion to planks, boards, and scantlings for supply to collieries, railway companies, docks, building and engineering trades. Fencing and gates, etc., were produced as well as timber articles for builders, carpenters and wheelwrights. Tinplate boxes were a specialist line for the South Wales trade. Mr. Cruse was one of the best known timber merchants in the west of England and resided for many years at "The Pines" in North Cary, where he died in 1909. His manager, David Gass, took over the business, which prospered, especially with the demand for timber during the two World Wars. He was also well known for his dialect literature under the pseudonym "Dan'l Grainger". The photographs, taken in 1929, show the sawmill and timber yard, and the horizontal saw in operation. *(photo Wm Hazell)*

Fronting North Street is the grand facade of "The Pines", for many years the residence of Jonathan Cruse. It has, like Ochiltree House, a brick front with stone quoins and architectual elements, fashionable instead of ashlar in the period around 1800. The finials on the adjoining walls significantly add to the atmosphere of grandeur. The photograph was taken in 1935.
(photo K. Alway)

C. PITHER & SON LTD.

Charles Pither began business in a small way in 1877, having served an apprenticeship to Mr. Druce, a cabinet maker of Clevedon. In 1898 he took over George Baker's long established furniture making business and transformed the premises for cabinet making on an extensive scale. The family business continued to grow with workshops and showrooms in Castle Cary, where "Pithers Emporium" was a notable feature of the market place, occupying the premises now occupied by Parkers, before moving to the Pithers Yard complex off the High Street. In addition to furniture and upholstery, the firm also sold carpets and linoleum, glassware and china, indeed it was the sole outlet for Cary crested china. Shops were opened in Yeovil, Crewkerne and Wells, and a removals arm covered the country. For a time an auctioneering facet was added to the business, but eventually dropped as the management concentrated on the core elements of its interest.

In the early 1900s George Moore's steam engine was employed to haul three or four trailers of furniture to the London warehouse and showrooms, a round trip taking about 10 days, or removals, as shown in the photograph from 1905.

By 1923 the concern was made into a Limited Company with the acquisition of Henry White and Sons of Yeovil, Charles Pither being appointed Chairman. On his death, his son John, inventor of the "Wunlock" - a device to lock the drawers of a bureau by closing the fall - succeeded as Chairman and ran the business until his death in 1948. John's sons Dennis and Jonathan (Roy) then took over, the latter as Managing Director, until the firm was taken over by the Tithe Barn Gallery Group.

The Pither family had very strong values both in their personal and business lives - Charles was a Quaker and John a lay preacher. They always guarded the welfare of their employees, and the entire staff of 50 in 1955 was covered by their pension fund. Many served the firm for their entire working lives, the last two working at Castle Cary when the business closed in the 1970s, namely Maurice Ridout and Jack Cooper had both been employees for nearly 50 years.

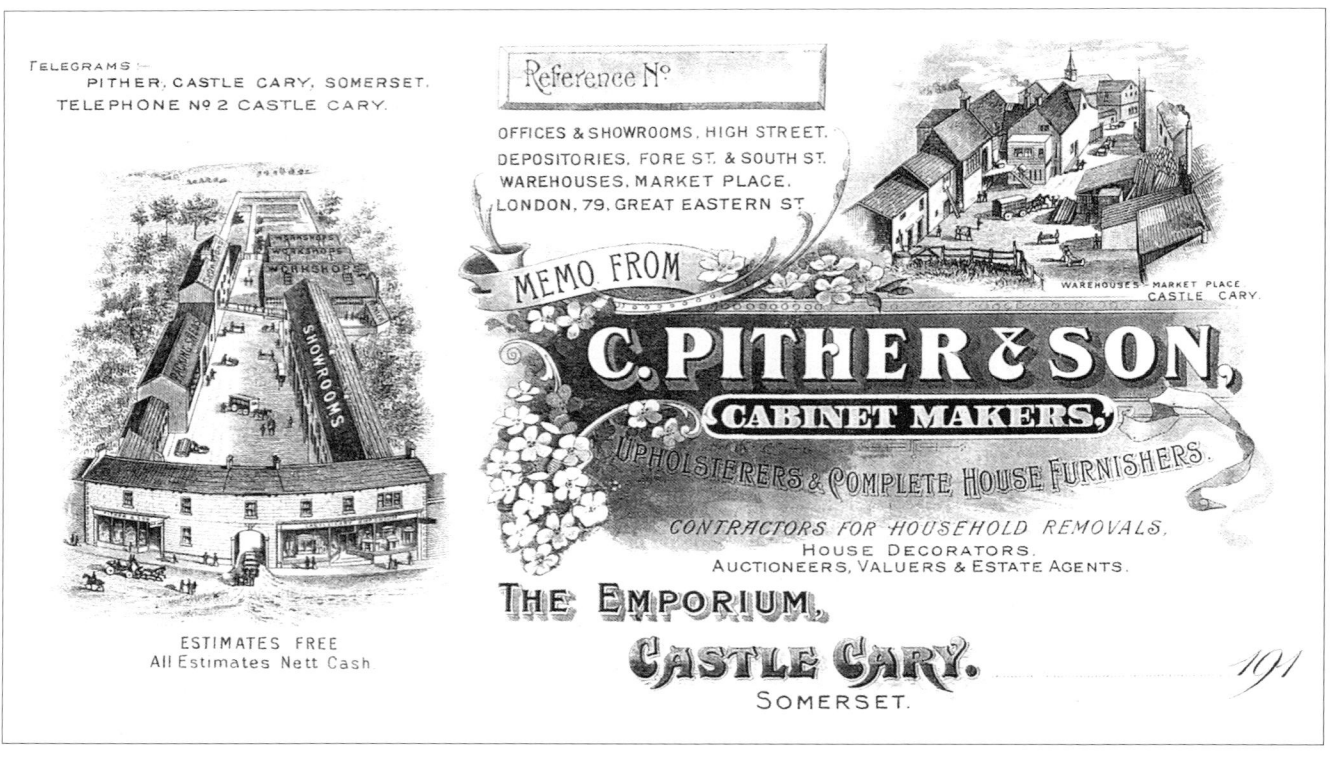

Pithers billhead showing the layout of the premises off the High Street.

Charles Pither, seated, second row from front, extreme right, and his son John, seated in the same row, extreme left, are seen here with their staff at the Castle Cary Emporium in 1905. The number of employees doubled as the business expanded over the following two decades. *(photo A. V. Pearse)*

Pithers Staff Outing, 1906.

An impressive spectacle - G. Moore's steam engine with the removal vans and staff on Bailey Hill c1905. *(photo A. V. Pearse)*

A SUMMER IDYLL.

Y ellow shone the sunlight down on glen and glade,
O ver fields and meadows two young lovers strayed,
U nderneath the lilac blossoms high above,
R ested they together, telling tender tales of love.
S uddenly the maiden to her stalwart sweetheart said :

"**T** hough you have my promise that we soon will wed,
R ecollect my happiness cannot be secure
U ntil you have told me something about our Furniture.
L et me tell you candidly the safest place to go—
Y ou will not find in Somerset a better one I know.

C heaper goods cannot be found anywhere around,
H eaps of bargains waiting from the ceiling to the ground,
A ll of first class quality, second hand and new,
R ich and poor are proving my words to be quite true.
L et us just consider, my dear, what we shall need,
E verything must be put down—a price must be agreed."
S o there upon the grassy mead the happy couple sat,—

P erhaps it was convenient, she wore a summer hat.
"**I** think we'll take the sitting-room, the maiden gently said
T here we shall want a couch and chairs, something like brother Fred,
H e only gave Six Pounds Fifteen at Pithers' famous store,
E ach piece is just as good as when it came inside the door ;
R emember, too, the carpet, his cost Two Pounds he said,

A nd that was several years ago, it's just the same as new,
N o need, my love, to say more here, our moments are too few,
D ear, we must go to Cary and see what PITHER'S do."

S o to the One Emporium the anxious couple go
O ne lovely day in sweet July—we'll leave them there I trow ;
N o household troubles mar *their* bliss, as we have cause to know.

C. Pither & Son, THE EMPORIUM, CASTLE CARY.

CYCLE INDUSTRY

During the last years of the nineteenth century and early part of the twentieth cycling became a very fashionable activity, exploited by Mr. T. Gosney who had introduced the cycle trade to Cary in 1884. From a humble start his business in Fore Street expanded to become one of the prominent examples of the industry in the west of England, producing the well known "Ivanhoe" cycle sold throughout the country and even exported.

He departed for Birmingham in 1915, but the cycle trade in Cary continued in the hands of R. Whitehead & Co and Jack Pike amongst others.

The periodical "Cycling" stated:- " 'Ivanhoe' cycles are really well made and deserving the attention of both wholesale and retail buyers. In the first place the finish is excellent, and incorporated in the machines are one or two very good 'talking points'. The fork crown is particularly strong; well designed, disc-adjusting, dust-proof hubs are fitted, and the compression stays are so arranged that a narrow tread is secured, whilst the stiffness of the rear frame is ample. By the method of combining crank and chain wheel, the gear can easily be changed in a few moments".

Mr T. Gosney

Ivanhoe Cycles & Motors.

Are you a Cycle or Motor Buyer?

If so, you are invited to call and see the latest novelties for 1903, which embrace many new features—Improvements which cannot fail to secure your appreciation. Then in the important matter of prices, we are able to "score" goals every time, and goods of the best quality at the lowest possible prices is what you desire, is it not?

Full Illustrated Price List Free.

DON'T FAIL TO SEE THE

'IVANHOE' MOTOR BICYCLE

Its capabilities unchallenged! Its merits proven!

Electric Charging Station.   Motor Inspection Pit.

Largest stock of HIGH-GRADE CYCLES and MOTORS in the West of England.

GOSNEY'S
Ivanhoe Cycle and Motor Works, CASTLE CARY.

"IVANHOE" CYCLES!!
First in 1884. Foremost ever since.
There are to-day (in Castle Cary alone)

Over 60 Satisfied Purchasers of Ivanhoe Cycles.
Comment is needless.

Illustrated Catalogue, with lamp-lighting table, post free.
"HUMBER" "RUDGE-WHITWORTH" & SINGER CYCLES
IN STOCK,

1899 BEESTON Pneumatic Cycles, quite new, £6 10 0 each
1899 Cushion Tyred Safeties, new, £4 18 6

Please note Prices and compare.   Hundreds of latest up-to-date Cycles in stock to select from.

GOSNEY'S "IVANHOE" CYCLE WORKS, CASTLE CARY.

"Ivanhoe" advert in Castle Cary Visitor, June 1899.
(A. V. Pearse)

CREED'S
Ivanhoe Cycle and Motor Works,
FORE STREET, CASTLE CARY.

ANY MAKE MOTOR OR CYCLE SUPPLIED,
Machines built Specially to Order.
Cycle Accessories of every Description.
Motor & Cycle Renovations.   Plating & Enamelling.
Estimates Given.
Agents for Enfield Cycles and Motor Cycles.
A.J.S., Triumphs, Swifts, Singers, and Morgan Runabouts.

All Sizes Motor and Cycle Tyres in Stock.

The Ivanhoe Cycle Works were eventually taken over by Tom Creed, who expanded the garage side of the business, which lasted until the 1950s. The site is now occupied by Phillips Garage.

Jack Pike stands in the doorway of his cycle shop near the Horse Pond during the 1940s.
(photo B. Lush)

TRADES AND BUSINESSES

Mineral waters were manufactured in Castle Cary from 1882 when William Poole founded his business next to the "Britannia Hotel". He sold the concern to his brother Thomas in 1884, who continued the operation until his death in 1906, after which it was carried on by his son W. T. Poole. Thomas was an enthusiastic supporter of the temperance movement, perhaps not surprisingly considering his business output! The area in front of the Poole's premises and the "Britannia" was not named "The Triangle" until 1914. The view dates from c.1904. *(photo A. V. Pearse)*

W. T. POOLE,
ÆRATED WATER MANUFACTURER,
CASTLE CARY,

Can now supply at very low prices all kinds of

Winter Cordials : Ginger and Cherry Brandy, Ginger Wine, Peppermint, etc., in Pint or Quart Bottles.

Several generations of the Clothier family were engaged in the rake-making trade at their workshop in Wyke Road until production ceased in about 1949 as a result of increasing modernisation of agriculture. Left to right are Harry Arthur Clothier and his father Edwin Clothier with examples of their hay rakes in the years before the First World War. The "Clothier Rake" was favoured by farm workers for its "lie" and made from a hazel handle with an ash head, obtained from local woods. The handles were steamed and turned on a lathe, and fitted to the heads which generally contained eleven teeth. The wholesale price for a rake was 1s 3d to 2s 0d. The family also produced hurdles and cribs for use by sheep farmers. *(photo Mr. G. Clothier)*

Charles H. Clothier (1918-1977) began his career assisting his father in the rake-making business but soon transferred to the building trade, establishing his own business in 1950, including chimney sweeping work. Other family members joined the business, including his wife Ida, son Graham and brothers Geoff, Cliff and Ken. From 1950 to 1958 Mr. Clothier ran his business from a lock-up garage at Torbay Road, before moving to "Fourways" at Ansford, a site of two acres without buildings. A carpenter's workshop was erected in which Seward Gregory and his team manufactured windows and doors etc. Eleven houses and bungalows were erected on part of the land, and with work increasing, in 1962 Mr. Clothier formed a Limited Company known as Chas. H. Clothier & Son Ltd. In 1963 Mr.Clothier purchased "Churchfields" between Ansford and Castle Cary and development was permitted, after some controversy, of approximately 200 houses and bungalows. After a further phase of construction, part of the site was named "Clothier Meadow" in 2001. The photograph taken in 1965 at "Fourways Close" shows the staff and workforce as follows: *Left to right, back row:* Peter Chinnock; Stan James; Edgar Restorick; Jack Stockman; Malcolm Chamberlain; Owen Cox; B. Clothier; Brian Harris; Brian Osborne. *Third row:* NK; Gordon Vaux; ? Hartnell; G. Toop; Bob Ashman; Geoff Greatwood; Ron Hatcher; Chris Dycer; Phil Marsh; Michael Wood. *Second row:* A. Haytor; Alan Golledge; Dave Eaton; Ted Tanner; Norman Foster; Harold Leader; Stan Palmer; Bill Gifford; Eric Shepperd; Ben Rowsell; Dave Close; G. Greatwood; Jim Chivers; M. Hamilton. *Front row:* M. Pullen; Ben Paul; Seward Gregory; Ken Clothier; Edna Sims; Chas. Clothier; Ida Clothier; Graham Clothier; Ray Dicer; Geoff Clothier. *(photo Mr. G. Clothier)*

A splendid example of a Victorian shop premises and frontage is seen in this 1905 photograph of Samuel Snook's business on the corner of Lower Woodcock Street and Station Road. The shop was established in the 1870s selling glassware, china and furnishing items. Samuel Snook also became a draper and outfitter; the window displays containing mainly flannel underwear, braces, shirts and other garments. In 1906 he began selling toys; and as Samuel Snook and Son the business continued until 1936. *(photo A. Appleby)*

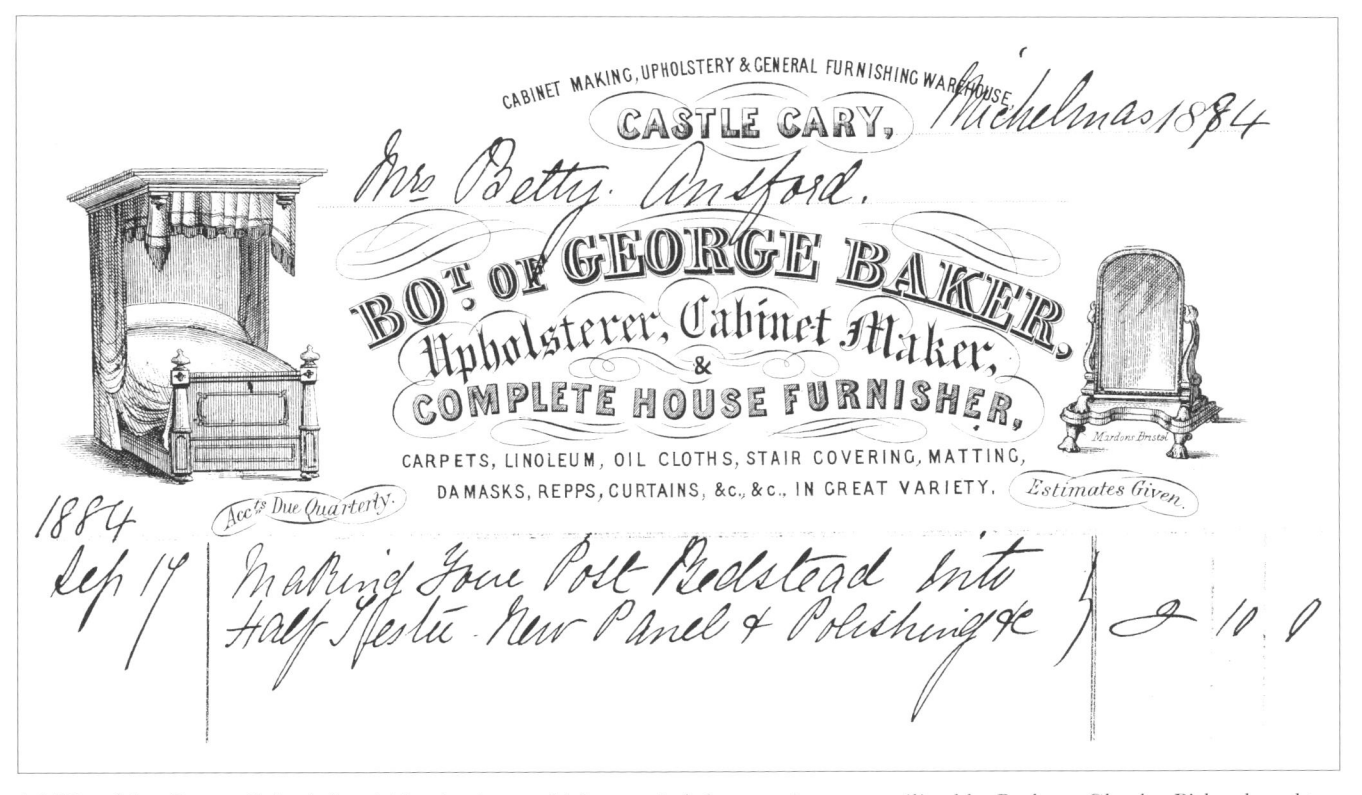

A billhead for George Baker's furnishing business which occupied the premises now utilized by Parkers. Charles Pither bought this concern in 1898. *(K. Wright collection)*

Fore Street was transformed during the nineteenth century as many buildings were re-built or re-fronted. Typical of the numerous low thatched cottages which were replaced is this example which stood on the site later occupied by Powell's butcher's shop built in 1882, and was the home of George Hicks, a shoe-maker. The photograph dates from the 1870s, shortly after the adjoining building on the left side had been re-built by Mr. W. Ellis, as a confectioner's shop and now the Co-op stores. Mr Powell's shop, with minor alterations to the frontage, is now the Keinton Bakery.
(photo Miss B. Laver)

William Taylor and his staff outside his shop in Fore Street in 1908 with the display of meat hung outside which was the usual practice at the time. Butchers were numerous in Castle Cary and in 1907 William Taylor succeeded to a business established by his wife's uncle, Mr. Powell, and under whose name it continued. Behind the shop was a slaughter house, reached through the doors on the right, a facility utilised by other Cary butchers. Livestock were herded from the street through to these rear premises, and evidently occasionally escaped. *(photo B. Laver)*

Eli Lush and his staff display their range of meat and game outside their elegant premises in the High Street, with the postman and townsmen in support. Previously a butcher's shop run by the Toogood family, then the Sharman family, the tradition continues with the current generation of the Lush family. *(photo B. Lush)*

A promotional photograph taken inside E. Lush and Son's shop in the High Street in 1970. *Left to right:* Janet Hutchfield (*née* Lush); Harold ("Annie") Sherrell; Gardinal Lush; Reginald Lush (retired) and Edwin (Ted) Lush.

Established 1851.

AUTUMN AND WINTER, 1905.

J. M. GREEN,

Draper, Tailor, Milliner and Dressmaker,

CASTLE CARY,

is now showing goods for coming season at exceptional prices.

CLOTHING CLUBS & CHARITIES SUPPLIED.

Flannelettes, Flannels, Blankets, Quilts, Sheets, and Furnishing Drapery bought at favourable prices.

DRESSMAKING. First-class fit and style guaranteed.

Mourning and Wedding Orders promptly executed.

MILLINERY OF EVERY DESCRIPTION

FUNERALS COMPLETELY FURNISHED.

Agent to the Norwich Union Life and Fire Insurance Societies.

OUTFITTING AND BOOT STORES

are now fully stocked with

Smart Rainproof Coats, Overcoats, Suits, Trousers, Youths' and Juvenile Clothing of every description.

Tailoring in all its branches.

Fit and style guaranteed.   Hundreds of patterns to select from.

Shirts, Ties, Collars, Hats and Caps in all the latest styles.

☞ **BOOTS AND SHOES!!** ☜

Over 2,500 pairs in stock at special prices for cash.

WATERPROOFS!

LADIES' AND GENTS'. BEST MAKES.
LOWEST PRICES.

AT

E. J. PARKER'S,

Tailor and Breeches Maker,

COSTUMIER, ETC.,

MARKET PLACE,

CASTLE CARY.

Also see our new Hygienic Self (Plaid) lined

RAINPROOF OVERCOATINGS

(not Rubber-proofed).

They make splendid Overcoatings suitable for rain or cold.

An attractive display to entice customers was a feature of E. A. White & Co's confectioners' shop in Fore Street as this example from the 1920s shows. In more recent decades the shop has been known as The Black and White sweet shop, but is now closed as a result of the owner's retirement.

"Francis House" in Fore Street was during the late 19th century the residence of Alfred Priddle, who ran a long established butcher's shop from the building. After his death the premises were acquired by Mary Jane Bettey who for a short time around 1902, ran the shop with her sister Georgianna as "fancy dealers", before letting it to Henry Close, who continued in the same line of business, as shown here in about 1910. The Appleby brothers took over the shop and ran it through the 1920s and 30s, until the Spearmans purchased it in 1940. Their business, selling toys, wool and stationery was a well patronized one, eventually taken over by the Ashmans. Since 1985 the shop has been Mrs. Maureen Higgins' pet shop, with a further part of the building operating as a travel agency. *(photo A. V. Pearse)*

C. MARTIN & SONS,
CENTRAL STORES,
CASTLE CARY,

Have the most complete stock of

Photographic Requisites

in the district, at prices which will be found to compete favourably with those of any other firm in the kingdom

CAMERAS in stock from **2/6** to **£3 10**

'KING' ¼-plate STAND CAMERA

is a very special line, possesses all latest improvements. We assert with the utmost confidence that it cannot be beaten at the price, which is **21/-**, or **20/-** net spot cash.

'HOLBORN GUINEA' ¼-plate Hand Camera

is as absolutely perfect as it is possible for an inexpensive instrument to be. Price—**21/-**, or **20/-** net spot cash.

Free tuition to purchasers.

Plates, Papers, and Chemicals (guaranteed fresh) in stock. Developing, Printing, Enlarging, etc., at competitive prices.

Schering's Adurol Solution 1/- & 1/9,
A perfect all-round developer.
Cartridge Developers, Pyro, Hydroquinone, Metol-Quinol and Adurol in stock.

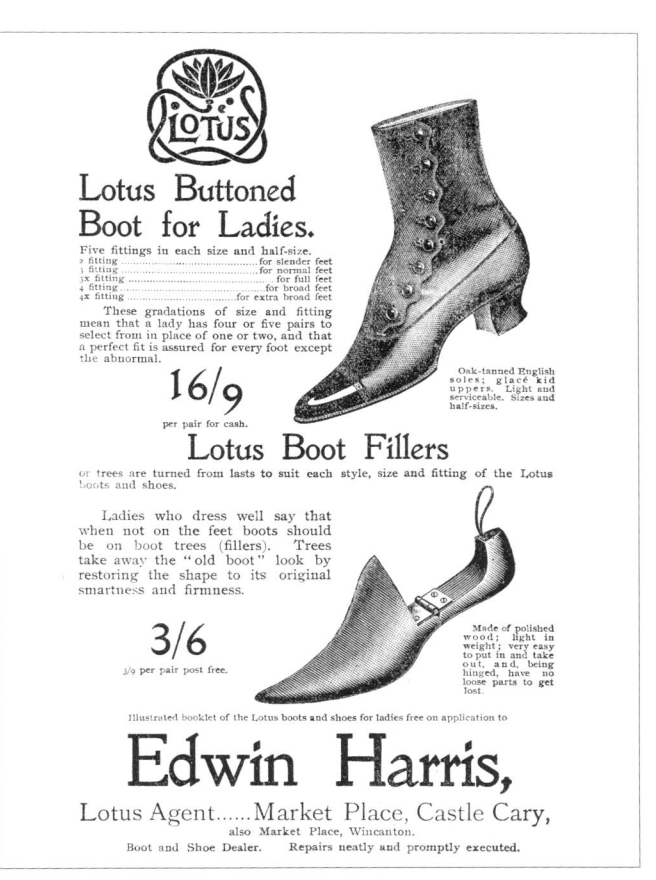

Lotus Buttoned Boot for Ladies.

Five fittings in each size and half-size.
2 fitting .... for slender feet
3 fitting .... for normal feet
3x fitting .... for full feet
4 fitting .... for broad feet
4x fitting .... for extra broad feet

These gradations of size and fitting mean that a lady has four or five pairs to select from in place of one or two, and that a perfect fit is assured for every foot except the abnormal.

16/9 per pair for cash.

Oak-tanned English soles; glacé kid uppers. Light and serviceable. Sizes and half-sizes.

Lotus Boot Fillers

or trees are turned from lasts to suit each style, size and fitting of the Lotus boots and shoes.

Ladies who dress well say that when not on the feet boots should be on boot trees (fillers). Trees take away the "old boot" look by restoring the shape to its original smartness and firmness.

3/6 3/9 per pair post free.

Made of polished wood; light in weight; very easy to put in and take out, and, being hinged, have no loose parts to get lost.

Illustrated booklet of the Lotus boots and shoes for ladies free on application to

Edwin Harris,

Lotus Agent......Market Place, Castle Cary,
also Market Place, Wincanton.
Boot and Shoe Dealer.   Repairs neatly and promptly executed.

The staff of Squibb's Garage, with Messrs. George and Montague Squibb in the centre, pose in front of the new showroom opened in 1953, fronting Station Road. At this time five brands of petrol were available. *(photo – Museum)*

John Frederick Squibb, pictured here on the left, was founder of the coachbuilders, wheelwrights and undertakers business in Station Road, later run by his son Frank, seen on the right of this view from 1914. The car is a "Star" - a luxury model for the year, complete with pneumatic tyres and electric lights, while in the background are carts and a box wagon, typical of the vehicles built by the firm. The premises were modernised to reflect the evolution of transport and survived until the site was cleared for housing development in 1987. *(photo Castle Cary Museum)*

Jack Norris stands outside his premises known as "Central Garage" situated at the Market Place end of Fore Street, in 1933. The son of a Hertfordshire baker, born in 1900, Jack Norris was employed at the garage in 1923 and later purchased the business which prospered for many years, interrupted by closure during the Second World War while he and his staff served in the Forces. The building is said to have been a coaching house during the seventeenth century, and since the closure of the garage in the late 1960s has been substantially re-modelled and now functions as Dave Marsh's ironmongery store. *(photo Mrs. M. Dunn)*

A Squibb's advertisement from 1925.

'Phone No. 20.

'Grams: "Squibb, Castle Cary."

Good going eh! If on our route and you are broken down
Assistance here, and first-class gear—the best within the town,
Right here is where you're treated fair, and never treated badly
Arrest your pace, and rest your face, you want some petrol sadly.
Great jobs or small—we handle all from sparking plug to tyre.
Escape your woes, and save your clothes, we'll do what you desire.

G. M. & W. SQUIBB,

Coach and Motor Works,

CASTLE CARY, Somerset.

New Cars of any make supplied.
Open and Closed Cars for Hire.
Accumulators charged on the Premises.

Agents for :
CHEVROLET, BUICK, ESSEX.

Demonstration Models in stock and all Accessories.

Chemist O. W. Pearce stands in the doorway of his chemist's shop in the 1940s. Formerly the shop was an outlet for J. H. Roberts, Ltd., printers and stationers, who were still operating from other parts of the building. G. B. Foulis operated Castle Cary's other chemist's shop in Fore Street. *(photo Mrs. S. Reed)*

During the 1950s and 60s Len Fennon used the premises as an electrical shop, having moved from Fore Street, and neatly adapted the surmounting sign board. The photograph was taken in the 1960s. *(photo Mrs. S. Reed)*

Castle Cary Chamber of Commerce outside the Market House in 1946. *Front row, left to right:* S. J. Phillips; W. J. Pitman; Ralph Otton; E. White; E. J. Parker; John Pither; T. Salisbury Donne; W. Wyatt; Harold Vaux; N.K.; Read. *Middle row, left to right:* White; Hubert Laver; Archie Creed; Dennis Pither; H. Spearman; E. Brewser; Jack Otton; Claude Newport; Bertie Hall; William Thomas; Charlie Cleal. *Back row, left to right:* Frank Parker; Ted Asher; George Yeabsley; J. R. Bulley; Bert Southway; Harold Pitman; Reginald Lush; W. Taylor. *(photo B. Lush)*

Arthur Parsons pictured in his greenhouse at Mill Lane Dairy in the 1970s. In addition to his local milk round he sold his home grown flowers, salad crops and vegetables. *(photo Mrs. S. Reed)*

W. H. Brake and Son operated a thriving dairy and tea room business opposite the horse pond, seen here in 1914.
(photo A. V. Pearse)

FRESHEST DAIRY PRODUCE.

For Immediate Deliveries (large or small) of

Fresh Churned Butter, Eggs, Cary Clotted Cream, English Cheddars, Cheddar Loaf. Any weight from 8 lbs. upwards. Give us a trial. Rock Bottom Prices. Distance no object.

ORDERS EXECUTED BY RETURN OF POST OR RAIL.

W. H. BRAKE & SON, The Dairy, CASTLE CARY, SOMERSET.

FOR ALL KINDS OF BOOT & SHOE REPAIRS

C. CLEAL,

BAILY HILL, CASTLE CARY.

All kinds of Rubbers, Laces, Polish, etc., in stock.

BOOTS AND SHOES MADE TO ORDER.

SCHOOLS AND CHILDHOOD

Southend Girls' School
CASTLE CARY.

Conducted by Miss M. C. Grosvenor, efficiently assisted by Resident Governesses and visiting Masters.

Limited number of Boarders received; Vacancies for two.

During the past 10 years 49 pupils have been successfully prepared for College of Preceptors, School Examination of the Associated Board of the Royal Academy and the Royal College of Music, Trinity College, and London College of Music. *Piano Practice of Juniors carefully superintended by Daily Junior Governesses holding 1st class Certificate, Intermediate Division, London College of Music.*

Continental French and German Calisthenics taught on the German system. Violin by Miss V. I. Chancellor, A.L.C.M. and M. Henri Riviere, who also gives lessons in Singing.

Next Term commences Sept. 19th.

For References and terms apply to

Mrs. or Miss Grosvenor.

Southend Girls' School was established by Mrs Sarah Grosvenor, wife of Rev. James Grosvenor, during the 1870s in South Cary, as a private school, catering for the daughters of mainly local tradesmen and farmers. The school prospered, and her daughter, Miss M. C. Grosvenor succeeded as principal on her mother's death in 1903, assisted by her father since 1895. New premises were adopted in 1907, and again in 1915 when the school moved to Scotland House. Boys were also admitted, as shown in this group from 1905. *Left to right: back (fifth) row:* NK; NK; NK. *Fourth row:* Miss Grosvenor, Bessie Barrett, Peggy Green; John Barrett; Madge Hill; Hilda Baker; Miss Lockyer. *Third row:* Janet Mackie; Winnie Gifford; Mary Green; David Hill. *Second row:* Hugh McKerrow; Edna Clark; Hugh Hill; Mr. Grosvenor. *Front row:* NK; Walter Chant; Jessie Vincent; John Vincent; Willie Barrett. *(photo A. V. Pearse)*

Castle Cary and Ansford National Schools from a view of 1903, were built in 1840 by R. Francis, to serve the two parishes, and much enlarged in 1850. They were largely re-built in 1876, to accommodate 380 pupils. They became a Board school in 1889, with Ansford building its own school in 1890. The infant school at Florida had closed in 1876 and its pupils had moved to the National Schools. In 1903 the school became known as the Council Schools, and combined juniors and seniors until 1940, with the building of the new school at Ansford, which took pupils over 11 years of age. Until 1935 boys and girls were taught in separate classes. The school is now known as Castle Cary County Primary School. *(photo Mrs. V. Nicholls)*

A group of girls of Standard 4 at Castle Cary Council School in 1906, mostly attired in the typical white pinafores of the period. *(photo B. Laver)*

Mrs. Joy Howard, Senior Teacher with her class in 1978 at Castle Cary Junior School. *(photo R. Howard)*

Pupils of Ansford Junior School gather for a group photograph in the late 1950s, with Mrs. Roberts, the Headmistress, to rear, right. The school, built in 1890, closed in 1967 and pupils transferred to Castle Cary primary School. *(photo P. Harrison)*

Ansford Secondary Modern School seen from Maggs Lane in 1948. Built during the Second World War on an 11½ acre site at a cost of £32,000, the school admitted its first pupils in 1940 before construction was completed. Mr. Henry T. Gough was appointed Headmaster with approximately 140 pupils, soon augmented by a further 150 evacuees and staff from Southampton, with initially local children attending during mornings and the evacuees during afternoons, until the groups were amalgamated. The school was surrounded by vegetable gardens where the boys were taught horticultural skills, and produced much of the vegetable requirements of the kitchens. The gardening master, Mr. Sam Steer's car, a Riley Eight, is shown in front of the buildings. During more recent decades the school has been considerably extended and now accommodates more than twice as many pupils as during the early years. *(photo P. Harrison)*

Ansford Secondary School Domestic Science class during the early 1940s. Practical skills formed an important part of the curriculum at this time. *(photo P. Harrison)*

Ansford School Staff 1947-48 – *Standing left to right:* Pam Stokes; John Harrison; Pat Etherington; Ron Collett; Mr Long; Hamilton Read; Doreen Hayes; Norman Smith; E. O. Brown. *Seated left to right:* Brenda Francis (secretary); Teg Phillips; Henry T Gough (Headmaster); Margaret Wickenden; Miss V. Brown. *(Photo Mrs Pat Harrison)*

Ansford Old Scholars netball team v. school team - 1949. *Left to right, back row:* Sylvia Palmer; Ruth Adams; Betsy Adams; Vera Bleek; Brenda Francis; Veronica Perrot; Mary Codling; Janet Lush; Pat Harrison. *Front row:* Sheila Champion; Marlene Goddard; Sheila Goodland; Eileen Bow; Beryl Wiltshire; Irene Carpenter; Pat Allen.

Beautiful Baby Competition 1952 – *Back row left to right:* Betty Helps (Gillian); Joyce Paul (Jenny); Janet Hutchfield (Richard); Clara Marsh (David); Joan Cave (Sandra); Mary Griffin (Norman). *Front row left to right:* Brenda Laver (Jackie); Elsie Targett (Jackie); Jean Cave (Janet); Heather Scholar (Diane); Jessie Cutler (Peter). *(photo Judy Marsh)*

Castle Cary Cubs on summer camp at Budleigh Salterton in 1959 with the Senior Scouts and helpers in the back row. *(photo Rowland Howard)*

The Scout and Guide Gang Show in 1972 on stage at Ansford School. For many years the Gang Show was one of the most popular events for the younger generation, with nearly 100, including the cubs and brownies, participating. *(photo V. Nicholls)*

The First Guide and Scout Band was formed in 1978 and is pictured here with Rev. Frank Hall in Castle Cary Parish Church.

Rowland and Joy Howard in 1998 on the presentation to the former of the Silver Acorn. *(photo R. Howard)*

Rowland Howard was born at Southampton in 1935 and on leaving school attended Sparsholt Agricultural College before coming to Somerset to work at Sutton in 1956. In 1962 he became Scout Leader at Castle Cary, a post he held for 20 years before becoming Group Scout Leader for three years, and District Commissioner from 1985 to 1995. In 1977 he started the Scout and Guide band, which he ran until 1997. He retired from A.D.C. Adult Support in 2000, aged 65, but remains Chairman of the District Scout Fellowship and Chairman of the Leader Appointments Committee. He was awarded the Silver Acorn in 1998. In addition to his scouting activities, Rowland is a Vice-President of the Carnival Society and a member of the Twinning Committee. He served as a Churchwarden at Castle Cary for 22 years and joined the choir on his retirement from this post in 1999. Joy Howard was born at Ditcheat in 1935 and spent all but three years of her life in Castle Cary. Educated at Miss Grosvenor's School, the Primary School and Sunny Hill, where she became one of the head girls, she trained as a teacher and took a post at Bruton before moving to Castle Cary Primary School. She met Rowland at a pantomime rehearsal in 1958; they were married at All Saints in 1960. She was Guide Leader at Castle Cary for 15 years, before becoming District Commissioner, a post she held for 10 years. Then she became County Adviser for Handicapped Guides and Brownies and District Secretary for the Scouts, and District President for the Guides. She was a J.P. from 1970, a member of the church choir and relief organist, a member of the P.C.C., leader of the Mothers' Union and Secretary of the Sunny Hill Old Girls Association for 27 years. She died in 1998.

CHURCHES

ANSFORD CHURCH

The Parish church of St. Andrew dates from the 14th century, but only the simple perpendicular west tower, in blue lias, remains from this structure of which no illustrations seem to survive. The remainder of the building was completely re-built and opened on 15th August 1861 at a cost of £1,000, raised partly by subscription, but largely the gift of the Woodforde family, holders of Ansford Rectory for over a century, and formerly as stewards of the Manors of Castle Cary and Ansford patrons of the living. The architect was C. E. Giles, and the work carried out by Castle Cary builder E. O. Francis, in Cary stone with freestone dressings. Two stained glass windows were erected to commemorate members of the Woodforde family; and the interior designed in typical Victorian ecclesiastical taste. From the old church were incorporated the late twelfth century font, the oak pulpit and two square-headed windows utilized in the porch. In 1889 an organ was presented by the Rev. Lewis Colby, an organ chamber having been built in 1898, and gas lighting was installed in 1906. The four bells, one of which pre-dates the Reformation, were re-hung in 1993, and two bells added. Renewal of the floor in the 1950s resulted in the removal of the pews.

In the churchyard is the now rather neglected stem of the old Ansford cross, rescued and erected on a stone base in 1904. New walls and gates had been erected in 1893 and land was given by the Barrett family to extend the churchyard in the 1960s.

South west of the church, near the gully in Churchfield, was St. Andrews's well, corrupted to "Tantrum's Well", taking its name from the dedication of the church. It was said that no water made such good tea, and was celebrated for curing maladies of the eyes and other medicinal purposes. It was formerly used in the baptismal font. In 1921 few traces of the well remained and since that time traces of it have been obliterated.

Ansford Church from the south in a drawing made in 1902. *(from postcard, V. Nicholl's collection)*

A view of Ansford church in a sylvan setting, from Churchfield c1900. *(photo K. Wright)*

The interior, with pews and lighting by oil lamps c1903. *(photo K. Wright)*

CASTLE CARY CHURCH

All Saints, Castle Cary, as it stands today represents the almost complete rebuilding of its 15th century predecessor during the mid-1850s in a more flamboyant style.

The architect was Benjamin Ferrey, of London, the Diocesan architect with several major commissions in Somerset, and the builder, a Mr. Davis of Langport. The church was lengthened by 15 feet, a new tower and spire were erected, a new north chapel built, the entire roofing renewed and galleries constructed on the north and south sides. A stone reredos was placed under the east window, the organ was re-modelled and new pews fitted. Brass gas fittings were introduced. Several stained glass windows were installed, the gifts of various benefactors. The total cost of the restoration was £3,500, and the re-opening ceremony took place on 8th August 1855.

From the earlier building remains the font, part of a piscina at the east end, a holy water stoup on the north side, part of the south door and porch, wood screens separating the north aisle from the vestry, the pulpit (excluding the carved figures), most of the pillars and arches, and part of the window mullions and tracery.

The early mediaeval settlement at Castle Cary was probably in the area around the church, of which nothing survives except perhaps the Norman font now preserved in the Town Hall. The perpendicular building, for which there are numerous records and illustrations, was subjected to considerable damage by Cromwell's and Fairfax's army which passed through and spent three days in the locality in 1645. The organ was demolished and carvings and ornaments defaced by the soldiery. As a result of their depredations it was necessary to re-cast the bells and re-lead the roof. The church continued to have a connection with military matters - the room over the porch, known as "Johnny Mountain's chimmer" was used for storing the accoutrements and powder belonging to the Militia into the 19th century.

The situation prior to restoration may be gleaned from "The Church Builder" of 1865. "From want of proper church room, and on account of the miserable condition of the church before its restoration, the people had become much dispersed and four dissenting meeting houses which had been recently erected were well filled. As in most cases church and parish had fared alike: and here both had been permitted to go sadly to decay. The church had been much disfigured by all sorts of awkward contrivances for obtaining more room: and not only was the building blocked up with old fashioned pews of all conceivable shapes, and possessing the utmost amount of inconvenience, but the whole fabric from base to spire was in a state of great dilapidation. The parish was hardly better off, for previous to the incumbency of the present Vicar, there had been no resident Vicar for nearly 200 years. Before its restoration, the church afforded accommodation for only 403 persons, and many of the seats were practically unavailable. There is now room in the church for 743 persons."

Canon Meade, an energetic figure responsible for the restoration of the church, also built the Vicarage on an adjoining site and largely at his own expense in 1846. Further work was undertaken on the church, notably a replacement organ installed in a new transept built on the south side of the church in 1891, and lining of the inside of the roof with stained boards in 1895. The churchyard was closed in 1898 and its role taken by the cemetery. One of the yew trees is a venerable specimen, dating to c1483.

The peal of six bells in Castle Cary church were restored in 1903 by Messrs. Taylor of Loughborough, the photograph being taken by G. Gyngell before they were raised to the belfry. *Left to right are:* Rev. E. H. Vaughan-Jones (Curate); a Taylors' workman; Rev. A. W. Grafton (Vicar); a Taylors' workman; C. Baker (Secretary to the ringers); D. W. Ash (Churchwarden); H. Harrold (Churchwarden); E. O. Francis (Sexton). The bells were re-dedicated by the Ven. F. Brymer, Archdeacon of Wells on 3rd December 1903 and their first use was tolling for H. C. Pitman, who had been killed in an accident while working in the belfry repairing the clock in late November. *(photo D. Biles)*

A sketch made in 1842 of Castle Cary Church before it was transformed by the re-building and enlargement of 1855. It had recently survived an attack by a maniac called King who had attempted to set fire to the building and had broken many of the windows. *(A. V. Pearse collection)*

Declining church attendance meant that by the 1950s the galleries were disused and futhermore had become badly affected by woodworm infestation. Miss Verdon Smith offered to pay the costs of their removal and when this was agreed a faculty was obtained and the work carried out by Thomas and Sons. *(photo K. Youings)*

A photograph of 1910 shows Ernie Creed of Dimmer, sometime Captain of the bell-ringers, standing at the top of the church spire which he ascended as the result of a bet for one pint of cider while the weather cock was being erected. Ironically the Creed family of Castle Cary were descendants of Rev. John Creed, Vicar from 1664–1721. He was not the first to perform such a feat – in 1896 Jacob Talbott climbed the spire and drank a glass of beer sat astride the weathercock. The tower has a height of 67 feet, and the spire 62 feet; a total of 129 feet. The pinnacles at the corner of the tower are carved at their bases with faces of Cary worthies - one being Harry Russ, a Castle Cary lawyer. *(photo Mrs. J. White)*

The Vicar, organist, churchwardens and choir of All Saints, c1948. *Left to right, front row:* C. Chambers; A. Chambers; K. Chambers. *Second row:* P. Lamb; M. Barber; J. Jefferey; D. Hart; R. Collings; J. Stokes; L. Stokes. *Third row:* Miss H. Poole; Miss I. Porter; Mrs. Cooper. *Fourth row:* R. I. Drewett (churchwarden); A. S. Hearn (organist); N. Legg; F. Davis; H. Newport; S. Kemp; C. Hoskins (churchwarden). *Fifth row:* J. Hart; Rev. Kemp; H. Collings; H. Meaden. *Back row:* A. Reeder; E. Ridout; W. Stride. *(photo K. Youings)*

A group including the first lady bell-ringers at Castle Cary, during the late 1940s. *From left, front row:* J. Ackland; Ern Creed (captain); J. Asher; H. Milburn; P. Sherrell. *Second row:* D. Curtis; W. Baber; M. Creed; H. Merrifield; S. Gifford; F. Simmonds; W. Tiley. *Back row:* A. Rapson; G. Creed; U. Phillips; M. Otton; H. Creed; NK. *(photo Mrs. K. Creed)*

THE METHODIST CHAPEL

Methodism had deep foundations in Castle Cary, indeed John Wesley visited the town on a number of occasions between 1784 and 1790. The first chapel was opened in about 1785 and was situated in Horner's, later Pither's, Yard and served for over fifty years before being sold and later demolished. The new chapel, seen here in a view from the late 1890s, was built by John Lane, of Doulting, from plans adapted from Shepton Mallet chapel. The foundation stone was laid 26th June 1838, and the building opened 23rd May 1839. A school room was constructed beneath the chapel itself, the earth being dug out and carted away by a band of volunteers. In 1874 it was decided to modernize the interior - the old high pews and pulpit were replaced, and a central chandelier substituted for gas brackets. The first organ was purchased in 1875. In 1889 a further renovation was undertaken, and a preacher's vestry erected, and additional sittings provided. The organ was replaced in 1895 and major work was done to the roof in 1899. Further modifications were made in 1914, when the organ was moved, choir stalls added, two new vestries built, and hot water heating installed. New windows were fitted and a lavatory provided, all for a cost of £550. The photograph also shows Castle Cary photographer Mr. G. Gyngell's studio to the right of the chapel. Wrecked by a gale in March 1905, it was replaced as a result of donations from townspeople, and survived until 1911. *(photo B. Laver)*

The interior is shown in a view from 1895, recovered from a deteriorating glass plate negative. The organ had just been installed, replacing the original instrument purchased in 1875 and for which the gallery had been extended. The debt on the new organ was paid off at the end of 1897, and the instrument removed to a new organ chamber behind the pulpit in 1914. It remains in use today. *(photo N. Foster)*

WARTIME

The two World Wars affected Castle Cary and Ansford directly, with the enlistment of personnel for the forces - in December 1915 for example 12½% of Castle Cary's population were in the armed services; by the direct result of enemy action as with the bombing of the railway station; with the utilization of the facilities of both agriculture and industry to support the war effort, and by the way that the wartime situation permeated every aspect of life, from rationing, fuel restrictions, blackouts and even removal of railings, to give but a few examples.

Castle Cary's involvement with the armed forces had a long history. Following the French Revolution in 1789 the possibility of invasion was considered a threat, and in 1794 a Robert Stevens was busy in Castle Cary and district raising a troop of gentlemen and yeomanry cavalry as part of a County Force. Castle Cary had the first voluntary Force to be formed, and consequently bore the number one on the uniform buttons. Arms and powder were stored in the room over the Church porch. Partial disbandment took place in 1801, but the force was re-established in 1803 as a result of the threat from Napoleon.

A new Volunteer Corps was formed in 1859, known as The Somerset Rifle Volunteers, an envisaged use being more the suppression of riots and tumults, should such occasion arise, as experienced in other parts of the country. Training was carried out on a regular basis, officers usually being members of the local gentry. The uniform was grey with blue facings. The Castle Cary force was on occasion 100 strong.

In 1887 the Castle Cary volunteers became part of the Somerset Light Infantry, a part of the Territorial Army, and in 1908 re-organization resulted in the amalgamation of the Castle Cary and Shepton Mallet Companies to form F Company of the Fourth battalion, The Prince Albert's Somersetshire Light Infantry. The uniform was red coats.

In 1912 a spacious Drill Hall was constructed by the Somerset Territorial Force Association at a cost of £3,000 in The Park in South Cary. It was opened on 27th September by Rt. Hon. Henry Hobhouse and included a rifle range, armoury, uniform stores, canteen, recreation room, etc.

The dark clouds gathering over Europe were soon to unleash the First World War, which took a heavy toll of the young men of Castle Cary and Ansford, with few families unaffected by the casualties. From Castle Cary 51, and from Ansford 15, were killed. The Territorials were sent to India. The war memorials constructed soon after the ending of the war are a lasting reminder of the impact of this conflict.

During the Second World War, with the threat of invasion a very real concern, the Home Guard was formed, with the North Barrow Force operating in much of Castle Cary parish, and including members from both Castle Cary and Ansford. Cary Home Guard was part of the 12th Somerton Battalion of the Somerset Home Guard, under the command of Maj. H. B. Clark O.B.E., M.C., Sgt. Maj. G. Dill was drill instructor. The Drill Hall was the local training heaquarters and there were look-outs on Lodge Hill and other prominent high spots. The rifle range was in the grounds of Hadspen House. The Home Guard was disbanded in 1944.

The War Memorial was unveiled on 11th November 1920 by the Marquess of Bath, seen here to the left of the cleric. Constructed of Cornish granite, and erected by Cary builders C. Thomas & Sons on a foundation of one hundred tons of concrete, all mixed by hand, it lists the 45 servicemen of Castle Cary who were killed in the Great War*; the 16 casualties from the Second World War being added later. The siting of the memorial in the Horse Pond necessitated the removal of the Jubilee Fountain, erected only 23 years before alongside the pavement in front of the Pond. (*An additional six were omitted.)
(photo A. V. Pearse)

Members of the Lush and Asher families in uniform during 1943. *From left:* Les Lush (air cadet); Ted Lush (scout); Reg. Lush (special constable); David Lush (cub scout); Harry Asher (special constable); Graham Asher (scout); Ken Lush (air cadet).
(photo B. Lush)

Damage at Castle Cary station after bombing on 3rd September 1942. The first 500kg bomb, at 9.15 a.m., wrecked the locomotive, engine no. 1729, an 0-6-0-T, and eight trucks of this goods train, damaged five other trucks and brought down the telephone wires. The second bomb demolished the signalbox, goods shed and parcels office and damaged further trucks, while a third destroyed the Railway Hotel and damaged three cottages and Prideaux's milk factory; a fourth fell in the River Brue. The station was also machine gunned, with casualties, three killed and ten injured. *(photo D. George)*

Frank Ridout of "Fairview Terrace" served in the Castle Cary Home Guard, and later with Allied Forces in the north African campaign. During the advance into Sicily he was killed through enemy action in August 1943 (aged 40) and given a military burial at Syracuse. *(photo Mrs. M. Ridout)*

North Barrow Home Guard which included men from Castle Cary and Ansford, were responsible for the majority of the rural area of Castle Cary parish, including the land around Dimmer Camp. Their knowledge of the landscape was considered an advantage. *Left to right, front row:* Ern Goodland; Rev. John Wright; Percy Boyer; Mr. Carr (Senior Officer); Jim Miles; Charlie Coward. *Back row:* Tom Goodland; Les Marsh; George Skinner; Alex Powell; Don Carpenter; Viv Marsh; Eddie Dauncey; Claude Lawrence; Ambrose Lawrence; Nat Higgins; Jack Wake; Bill Shires. *(photo V. Marsh)*

A photograph taken in September 1944 of the last parade of the Castle Cary and Ansford Home Guard, which took place in "The Triangle" between the War Memorial and the "Britannia Hotel". The Drill Instructor was Sgt. Major George Dill. Note that "YEOVIL" had been painted out of the advertising sign on the "Britannia". Early in the war, finger posts, road signs, farm wagon name boards, etc., were all removed or painted over to confuse enemy forces, though in fact the Luftwaffe had already undertaken a comprehensive aerial survey of the country. *(photo Mrs. J. Sweet)*

Home Guard cessation *(photo N. Dill)*

'Though the Home Guard is dying out,
Hitler—old man—we were on the look-out :
You tried your best by air and sea,
But the Home Guard was ready
And waiting for thee !

In Loving Memory

OF

THE CASTLE CARY

HOME GUARD

Who fell asleep on Sept. 11th, 1944

(with a possibility of a temporary revival)

Aged 4½ Years.

Thy Name Liveth for Evermore.

One of several air-raid shelters surviving in Castle Cary from World War Two, built of brick.

An aerial view taken in 1977 of the Dimmer Ammunition Dump facility constructed during the Second World War, now part of the Wyvern Waste Site. The photograph also shows extensive areas of mediaeval arable strip cultivation preserved as ridge and furrow, in blocks known as furlongs, especially between the above site and Alford, which is at the top (north) of the area shown. *(photo Wyvern Waste)*

At Dimmer was a major ammunitions storage facility built in 1939. The embanked and camouflaged bunkers were connected to the rail system, allowing the munition trucks to be loaded and unloaded directly outside the storage area. The photograph was taken in 1970: since then the structures have been levelled though part of one remains covered by a steel frame building. *(photo R. Lush)*

PERSONALITIES

James Taylor, M.D., was a noted medical practitioner in Castle Cary and the surrounding district during the middle decades of the 19th century. He was the natural son of his predecessor, Dr. Knight, and at an early age was taken into his father's household as a servant. His abilities soon became apparent and he was educated in the medical profession, achieving M.R.C.S.Eng: L.S.A. (1834), and M.D. (St Andrews 1847). Throughout his residence at Dr. Knight's, neither he nor his half sisters had any knowledge of their true relationship, and it was only when a growing affection between James and one of his sisters was observed, that it became necessary for the secret to be revealed. Dr. Taylor was involved in many of the affairs of Castle Cary, and became the first chairman of the Gas Company, formed in 1853. He lived on Bailey Hill, in the house which became the Post Office in 1882, a function which it retains. He died in 1867. Details of one of his cases have survived in the diary of Eliza Golledge, of Wraxall, for 1864, revealing the enormous difficulties faced by Victorian doctors in the treatment of serious illnesses. Photo taken by Castle Cary photographer F. S. Moore.
(photo A. V. Pearse)

William Macmillan was born in Wincanton in 1844, son of John Macmillan who had migrated from Ayrshire in 1826 to work in the local textile industry. Aged four, he was taken to Birmingham by his parents, and only returned in 1867 to join John Boyd's horsehair business. He became company accountant and later secretary, and on the death of his employer in 1890 took over the running of the business and resided at Ochiltree House. He was also Registrar of Marriages, a J.P., and a Somerset County Alderman. An enthusiastic antiquarian and entomologist, he founded a monthly magazine in 1896 known as the "Castle Cary Visitor", which contained local news and a fascinating collection of historical, topographical and natural history information. He continued to edit and publish this magazine until his death in July 1911, after which his children took up the reins until wartime conditions brought about its termination in December 1915. As a valued record of life in Castle Cary and district, it is perhaps his greatest memorial. *(photo Castle Cary Visitor)*

Douglas Macmillan was born in 1884 at Ochiltree House, son of William Macmillan. He was educated at Sexey's School, Bruton, walking there daily, and after leaving school he worked for the civil service in the Ministry of Agriculture. In 1912 he founded the first cancer relief charity in memory of his father who had died of cancer in 1911. It later became the Macmillan Fund and is very well known today. He was awarded the MBE in 1944.

A Barret Bros. billhead. Wosson Barrett used it to court Elizabeth Amelia Bettey (Bessie). They were married in 1884 at Ansford.

Wosson (originally Wason) Barrett (1849-1930) was the fourth of six sons born to William, a blacksmith, and Mary Barrett of West Lydford. His brother Sidney was apprenticed to William A. Ellis, confectioner, of Fore Street, Castle Cary, and Wosson came to Castle Cary in 1873 and joined him in the purchase of Mr. Ellis's business. The shop (now the Co-op) had been re-built by Mr. Ellis, and was adjoined on the north east by premises recently built by Charlie Butt and a thatched cottage occupied by Arthur Clothier, a shoemaker. Both of these were purchased and the latter demolished and rebuilt in 1890, and opened as grocery and pork butcher's departments; the original shop remaining as a bakery and confectionery operation, including a wine and spirits licence. Their business prospered, and the brothers purchased numerous properties in Castle Cary, including Church Villa, Ansford House, Villa and Cottage and Woodcock House and the property opposite their shops, where they erected Cavendish House in 1882 and three adjoining cottages in Woodcock Street in 1896. They introduced electric light to Castle Cary in November 1897. Wosson married his cousin Elizabeth Amelia Bettey, of Lower Ansford, in 1884. His partnership with Sidney was dissolved in 1904, thereafter Wosson operating the grocery and pork butcher's establishments, Sidney the confectionery shop, which was taken over by Wosson's son Robert W. H. Barrett in 1919 on Sidney's death. Wosson's shops were run by his son Wilfred after his death, the business lasting until 1939.

A very long established tailoring business in Castle Cary was that founded by Charles Churchouse in about 1820. Born near Weymouth in 1798, the son of a tailor, he married three times and had eleven children at Castle Cary. Joseph Churchouse (1841-1910) was the tenth child and eventually succeeded his father in the business. He married Amelia Melhuish (1842-1911) and they had a daughter and two sons: the elder, William, born in 1873, established a tailoring concern in Gillingham before emigrating to Canada. His brother Ernest (1880-1970) was apprenticed to the trade in London before returning to Castle Cary, where he ran the prospering business in Fore Street. There was plenty of competition, not only from several other tailoring shops - Messrs. D. Ash; H. Fowles; E. Parker; and J. Green but also from travelling "Scotch" drapers operating from the town. Ernest visited markets at Gillingham, Yeovil, Sparkford, Frome, Wincanton and Shepton Mallet, where he established a clientele amongst the farming and hunting fraternity. He married Amelia Lyford and they had three children. On his retirement in 1964, the business was sold to Mr. Parker.

Joseph Churchouse (1841-1910).
(photo Miss V. Churchouse)

Ernest Churchouse (1880 - 1970).
(photo Miss V. Churchouse)

CHURCHOUSE & SON,

TAILORS ✠ AND ✠ BREECHES ✠ MAKERS,

FORE ST., CASTLE CARY,

are now showing very special lines in **DRESS SUITS,**

TILLEY & HENDERSON'S NOTED DRESS SHIRTS,

A very smart lot of **DRESS TIES** quite new,

A good assortment of **GLOVES**, etc.

OVERCOATS in great variety at **astounding Prices !!**

If you want a reliable **WATERPROOF** C. & Son supply them, second to none in price and quality.

Style and Fit Guaranteed.   *Agents for best makes of Waterproofs.*

Advertisement, Castle Cary Visitor, Dec. 1898.

Tom Trowbridge, a native of Wiltshire, came to Wraxall in 1928 to work for a relative, and in the following year accepted an offer from Joe Tullett to work as an assistant in his drapery and outfitting business in Fore Street, established in 1909. After service in the RAF, part of which was in Africa, he returned to Castle Cary and in 1946 went into partnership with Freddie Neck to succeed the late Mr. Tullett, and in 1949 took over the whole business, which became a well known Castle Cary enterprise. In his spare time Tom developed an interest in music, becoming proficient with the violin, piano and eventually the church organ. He was appointed organist and choirmaster at Castle Cary church in 1960 and built up a large choir. The making of corn dollies was another favourite pastime. After 50 years in the drapery trade, he retired in 1979, and his business was acquired by Mrs. K. Lyons. He died in 1993.
(photo Mrs. V. Nicholls)

The firm of Woodforde and Drewett, Solicitors, had its origin in a practice founded by a member of the Woodforde family during the eighteenth century. The last Woodforde was Randolph, seen in the photograph of 1898, with Richard Blackway Drewett, who came to Castle Cary in April 1882 and entered the former's office. R. B. Drewett was admitted a Solicitor in 1911 and then became Mr. Woodforde's partner. He in turn took his son Richard J. Drewett into partnership, later joined by his son John. The family were prominent in many aspects of the life of the town, and the firm now prospers with the title Dyne Drewett.

Randolph Woodforde, seated and Richard Blackway Drewett, standing, taken in 1898. *(photo Dyne Drewett)*

The staff of Woodforde and Drewett in 1955. *Left to right:* Ernie White; Beryl Higdon; Esme Wade; R. J. Drewett; Norma Howard; Joyce Cooper; John Jones. *(photo Dyne Drewett)*

A prominent figure in Castle Cary, John Pither was the son of the founder of the furnishing business, Charles Pither. He expanded his father's business and took on many public offices, including membership of the Parish Council and as a Methodist Lay Preacher. He founded the well attended Young Men's Bible Class which met throughout the 1920s and 30s and was an active proponent of the Liberal cause in local politics. He also became a well known local auctioneer. *(photo K. Youings)*

Ralph Otton, shown here with his motorcycle, originally worked for Pithers and then started his own business in 1901 at Fairview Terrace, as a picture framer and house furnisher. More room was required so he constructed the shop premises which survive, facing Station Road, in 1908. From here he was able to sell a wide range of items, such as bedsteads, linoleum, carpets, blinds and perambulators. He was very enterprising in the invention of modes of conveyance for his stock in trade. During the 1920s he exploited the rapid spread of the wireless and moved into the radio and electrical business. In 1946 he moved to premises in Fore Street near the Horse Pond, formerly occupied by David Ash. His son Jack continued to run this business, which lasted into the 1990s, operated by his son Roger. *(photo R. Otton)*

William James Garland was born at Pylle in 1889, and served in the Somerset Light Infantry in France in World War I, returning, severely gassed, to a post with Cary cheese factors James Mackie and Sons, where he worked until his retirement. Throughout his life he was fully involved in the local community. He was a Director of the Market House Company and a Castle Cary Parish Councillor for 30 years, for 10 of which he was Chairman. In addition he served as Chairman of the Governors of Castle Cary Primary School and as a Governor of Ansford Secondary Modern School. As a life long member of the Methodist Church, he engaged fully in the local organization and held most of the offices connected therewith. He was also involved with the Liberal Association, and various children's charities. He lived in Torbay Road and died in 1964. *(photo M. Whatley)*

Theodore Rossiter was born in 1883 at Welton near Midsomer Norton and later moved to Ansford. He started a family builder's business in 1917 and was eventually joined by his sons Ralph and Arthur, who took over the concern as Rossiter Brothers. Ralph built his own house, "Rossgreen" opposite the end of Tucker's Lane, and their yard, now Stockman's. *(photo Miss T. Rossiter)*

PUBLIC SERVICES
POST OFFICE

Castle Cary Post Office, seen here during the 1920s, has occupied this elegant building with its pediment and Venetian window on Bailey Hill since 1882. Prior to this date it had been housed in a variety of premises, including the George Hotel from 1793 to c1811; a building on the east side of Woodcock House; the shop now occupied by Martins Stores; and before the final move, the building which was rebuilt as Stuckeys, now the National Westminster Bank. In 1842, the then postmaster, James Edwards, was transported as a result of the loss of a £5 note. *(photo A. V. Pearse)*

Miss Beatrice Bargery (1887-1969) grew up in a cottage near what is now "The Two Swans", in due course looking after her elderly parents. During the First World War, with most of the younger men in the forces, she was offered a job as Castle Cary's first post-woman, hence the No. 1 on her lapel badge. Her round included the area towards Alford and Lovington, for which she was provided with a bicycle. Indeed, a train traveller complained to the G.P.O. that such a mode of conveyance in the conduct of her duties was unseemly. The end of the war terminated her employment at the Post Office and she then delivered newspapers. *(photo K. Cross)*

Postal staff outside the Post Office in 1982.
Left to right: Bert Motson; Mrs. Nicolson; Jack Sweet; Norman Dill; Ernie Dill; Kerstin Cross and Postmaster Mr. Nicolson. On their retirement the Nicolsons emigrated to Australia.

Norman Dill with the Royal Mail van delivering and collecting from Castle Cary Station in the 1950s.

Jack Sweet was a popular local postman, seen here on the day of his retirement in April 1985. Apprenticed to the Pithers upholstery department, he left age 17½ to join the Royal Navy, and after demobilization returned to Pithers where he remained until 1950. He then joined the Castle Cary postmen. Associated with the local Scout movement, he enjoyed participation in Gang Shows and Pantomines. *(photo V. Nicholls)*

FIRE BRIGADE

Fire engines have been established at Castle Cary since the late 18th century, and with numerous thatched buildings in the area, were in frequent demand. An engine was long kept in a purpose-built shed near the horse pond. A purpose-built Fire Station was built and opened in 1959 near the church, and operates as a retained station with twelve retained firemen. About 100 calls a year are answered.

During the 1940s the three Castle Cary crews of six men trained at Wincanton until Castle Cary Fire Station was opened, with each crew on a sleeping duty one night per week. In this group, pictured at Wincanton are: *left to right, front row:* G. Stockley; W. Davis; L/F. P. Thomas; Stn. Officer C. Blinman; T. King. *Back row:* NK (Wincanton); NK (Wincanton); L/F. T. Brake; E. Fussell; L. King; C. Newport. *(photo M. Snelling)*

Castle Cary's Fire Station was opened by the Lord Lieutenant of Somerset, Col. Barnes, on 25th July 1959. The Officer standing with his back to the door is the Chief Fire Officer, Taunton, A. Bullion, and the row to the right facing forward includes: *from left:* Station Officer P. Thomas; L/F. T. Brake; E. Fussell; L. King; L. Powell; F. Garland; Monty Squibb; Tom Biss; R. Drewett; D. Norman. *(photo M. Snelling)*

Castle Cary Fire Brigade in 1984, with: *left to right, front row:* G. Clothier; J. Graham; A. Price; J. Higgins; J. Garland. *Back row:* R. Harris; M. Warren; D. Marsh; B. Harris; R. Rawson; G. Greatwood. *(photo D. Marsh)*

BRITISH RED CROSS

The Castle Cary Red Cross was formed in 1938, with ten men and W. M. Thomas as the first Commandant. The Women's Detachment was formed during the Second World War. The first ambulance, an ex-army model, was acquired in 1945, with H. F. Laver as Transport Officer, and manned on a rota system. A. H. Cox was the first full time driver, appointed in 1948. During the 1950s staff numbers increased and the County Council built a new Ambulance Station. C. P. Toop succeeded as Commandant in 1960, a post he held until promoted to Director of the Wincanton Division in 1972. He instigated the building of a new Red Cross Centre in Station Road, completed in 1969 and known as Fountain House, after a benefactor. The Castle Cary team operated over a wide area, including the Glastonbury Festival at Pilton and the Royal Bath and West Show.

Castle Cary Red Cross personnel, May 1960. *Left to right, front row:* Freda Pearse (nee Groves); NK; Mrs. Angel; Mr. Thomas; NK; NK; Mollie Fussell (nee Orchard). *Back row:* Edgar Warr; Bert Laver; John Bashford; Tom Moores; Jim Moores; Mr. Proctor; Cyril Toop; Victor Chamberlain; Jim Cox; Alec Tiller; Ernie Attwell. *(photo Mrs. Beesley)*

Castle Cary was represented at the British Red Cross Society Service of Dedication at St. Pauls Cathedral on 24th May 1972 by, *from left:* Tom Moores; Valerie Norton and Bert Lodge. *(photo R. Lodge)*

The Lord Lieutenant of Somerset, Sir Walter Luttrell, presenting the B.E.M. to Cyril Toop for his services to the Red Cross in 1982. *(photo Red Cross)*

Presentation to Mrs Pat Strickland and Mr. Cyril Toop in May 1980 outside the new Red Cross Centre in Station Road with Dr Audrey Dunlop (left) and Mrs Rosemary Beesley (second left). *(photo Mrs Beesley)*

TRANSPORT

Seen here is Jim Weeks' well turned out equipage in Gashouse Lane, later renamed Victoria Road. Jim Weeks had a profitable trade transferring passengers between the railway station and the town. The photograph is from a glass plate negative of about 1890 and a rare survival. On the east side of the lane was the Cary Gasworks, built in 1854, and on the west the Cary Brickworks, this site being replaced by Squibb's coach and motor works. *(photo N. Foster)*

An Aveling Barford road roller of 16 tons weight working in Castle Cary in the 1890s, part of a fleet of such plant operated by W. W. Buncombe of Highbridge throughout the West Country. The horse is pulling a water tank to refill the engine boiler. Between jobs the engine would tow a water cart and an iron wheeled living van to house the driver during the period away from home. Cary roads at this time were constructed of rubble topped with crushed stone. During the decade before WW1 the practice of spraying the surface with tar commenced. *(photo B. Lush collection)*

Herbert D. Creed was a farmer and miller, operating from Torbay Mills, adjoining the Higher Flax Mills, and utilizing steam and water power. His delivery cart, shown here in Station Road in 1912, was probably loaded with bran. Note the mechanism for operating the brakes. *(photo Golledge family)*

Arthur J. Parsons was a dairyman who initially sold milk around Castle Cary by the traditional means of dipping it from a churn for the customer. He was the first to establish a milk bottling plant and shown here is his motor delivery vehicle in the 1920s. *(photo N. Weeks)*

Jack Norris on his B.S.A. motorcycle in the Upper High Street in the late 1920s. *(photo M. Dunn)*

A Morris Cowley Saloon, YD 1804, sold by Squibb's Garage in 1931 had an eventful life. In 1963 it was at Brook House Inn, owned by Mrs. Mary Foster, and was later sold at auction. It is now at Chard, and restored to original condition. *(photo N. Foster)*

Ivy Norris in a Morris Cowley, c1920, 15.50 c.c. max speed about 55 mph, outside the Norris's home in Upper High Street. *(photo M. Dunn)*

Jack Norris driving a charabanc on an outing to Gough's Caves at Cheddar in 1922. *(photo M. Dunn)*

Squibb's rescue truck, with Dick Dunford driving, in about 1936. *(photo Museum)*

From the golden age of motoring - or what in retrospect seems to have been - comes this view taken in Lower Ansford in October 1936, which encapsulates the rosy view of the English countryside seen in the films of the period. The orchard on the left has since been replaced by bungalows, and most of the thatched cottage demolished. The group includes the "Times" photographer (who had come to take photographs of cider making) standing in the car, and his family; with Jack Barrett (in cap), to left, Sarah Barrett (standing on running board) and Madge Barrett (with hand on car). *(photo A. V. Pearse)*

SPORTS

CASTLE CARY BOWLS CLUB

In March 1984 an open meeting elected a committee empowered to form a bowling club. Mrs Ida Peaty donated a plot of land behind Florida House sufficiently large for a clubhouse, car park and spacious green, and work commenced in May 1985.

The new clubhouse and bowling green were opened on 2nd May 1987 by the Club President, Mrs. Peaty, who bowled the first wood. Rowland Derrett was Chairman, and the membership was about 130. Since 1990 the Club has been on tour most years, including visits to Cornwall, Oxfordshire, Herefordshire, Sussex and South Wales.

Members of the Castle Cary Bowls Club on 2nd May 1997 in front of the clubhouse on the tenth anniversary of the opening of the Club. *(photo D. & N. Legg)*

CASTLE CARY AND ANSFORD CRICKET CLUB

The Cricket Club is the oldest sporting club in Castle Cary, and one of the oldest in Somerset. It was formed as the Castle Cary and Ansford Cricket Club on 2nd May 1837 with Dr. W. E. Miller as President, but in 1840 combined with Bruton and Wincanton players to form the Hadspen Cricket Club, which survived until 1859, when the Castle Cary Club was re-formed, though it retained its headquarters at Hadspen until 1869. In 1870 matches were played on a field off South Cary Lane: a move was made to Catherine's Close in 1891.

The Club went on tour, firstly to the Isle of Wight in 1894, then the Isle of Man in 1895, the Channel Isles in 1896 and Lake District in 1897. Many other tours followed, until the outbreak of the Second World War closed the Club for the duration. The Club also entertained the M.C.C.

In 1945/6 the Club resumed its activities, the ground being named the Donald Pither Memorial Field, and John Pither became President. He was succeeded by S. J. Phillips, R. J. Drewett, J. R. Bulley, P. D. Boyer, E. Asher, E. Rayes, J. Harrison, M. Squibb and W. Webber. High standards continue to be maintained and the Club has an active following.

Castle Cary cricket team in 1958 outside the pavilion. Front row, from left: Ted Lush; Ron Dunford; M. Prout; John Harrison; Brian Robinson. *Back row, from left:* Arthur Martin; Ron Hunt; Richard Aubertin; John Drewett; Eddie Clothier; Robin Spearman. *(photo R. Hunt)*

An early view of the cricket field taken about 1900 showing the second pavilion, with Ansford Inn and Ansford House in the background. John Pither gave the Memorial Field to the Parish in April 1945 in memory of his son Donald who died in 1944 aged 26. Donald had been an accomplished sportsman, scoring 1400 runs in 1938 when aged 20. Castle Cary Cricket Club was given the right to use the field in perpetuity. *(photo B. Lush)*

Castle Cary Cricket Team Second Division - Champions of Yeovil Evening League Cricket in 1968.
Front row, from left: Steve Close; Paul Sherell; Mike Payne; John Hamer; Jack Pitman. *Back row, from left:* Ted Jones; Joe Trott; Ron Hunt; Walt Webber; Fred Trott; Dick Aubertin; N.K.; Gwynn Phillips; Paul Burcher. *(photo:- R. Hunt)*

CASTLE CARY ASSOCIATION FOOTBALL CLUB

The Football Club began in 1894 and was known as the "Non-cons", owing to its association with the Congregational and Wesleyan Sunday Schools. Matches were played regularly until the outbreak of the First World War, when like many other sporting clubs it was disbanded until the end of hostilities in 1918. Re-formed, the club was active between the wars, playing in various modes of strip, including hobnail boots, and was duly disbanded in 1939, with the onset of the Second World War.

In 1945 a scratch team was gathered and friendly matches organized, and in the 1946-47 season the club was re-formed with John Pither as Patron, W. W. Macmillan as President, Frank Parker as Chairman, Herbert Hall, Treasurer, Ken Clothier and Bill Peaty, Joint Secretaries. Home matches were played on the Donald Pither Memorial Ground, with headquarters at The Britannia Hotel. Strip was shirts of emerald green, and white shorts. The team played in the Yeovil and District and Blackmore Vale Leagues and was for many years under the guidance of Les King, Secretary for 21 years.

The club has continued to prosper, and in one season won seven cups. It now plays in the Somerset County League (Premier Division), the highest league in its history. The strip is now red shirts, red socks and white shorts. S. Blacker is President; Neville Hartnell, Chairman; Joe Trott, Secretary and Martin Barnes, Captain.

Castle Cary Association Football Club 1946-47. The team assembled for the first game played after World War Two against Yeovil Baptists, played at Yeovil on 31st August 1946. The result was Castle Cary 6, Yeovil 0.
Front row, from left: Ken Clothier; Ernest Dill; Jim Cox (Captain); Gerry Toms; Mons Helps. *Middle row, from left:* John King; Albert Francis; Ken Lush; Bill Brown; R. Braxton; Joe Francis; Bill Davis. *Back row, from left:* Bill Peaty; Reg Lush; Ernest Stockman; Les King; Tom Biss.

FIXTURES 1946-47

Date		Opponents	Where Played	Goals F.	Goals A.	Date		Opponents	Where Played	Goals F.	Goals A.
Aug. 31	Y	Yeovil Baptists	Away	6	0	Dec. ~~25~~ 26		~~ALWESTON (FINAL)~~ A&HS		0	1
" 31	F	I.A.D. Alford	Home	11	4	" 26	Y	Sparkford & Queen Camel Utd.	Home		
Sept. 7	Y	Odcombe	Away	6	3	" 28	Y	Milborne Port	Away	1	2
" 7	F	Templecombe	Home	0	7	1947			HOME		
" 14	Y	Montacute	Home	5	1	Jan. 4	B	Charlton Horethorne	~~Away~~	10	0
" 14	F	Evercreech Rovers	Away	0	8	" 4	F	~~Shepton Mallet A.T.C.~~	~~Home~~		
" 21	Y	Hambridge & Westport Utd.	Away	2	1	" 11	B	Evercreech Rovers AWAY	~~Home~~		
" 21	F	R.N.A.S. Yeovilton	Home	3	4	" 11					
" 28	B	Charlton Horethorne AWAY	~~Home~~	3	2	" 18	Y	~~St. John's Gym, Yeovil~~	Away		
" 28						" 18	B	Blackmore Vale Charity Cup (Semi-Final)			
Oct. 5	Y	~~Bradford Abbas~~	~~Home~~			" 25	Y	Keinton Mandeville	Away		
" 5	B	Wincanton Town (1st Rd. Merthyr Guest Cup)	Home	2	0	" 25					
" 12	B	~~Evercreech Rovers~~ TEMPLECOMB	Away	1	3	Feb. 1	B	Evercreech Rovers (McCreery Cup—1st Round)	Home		
" 12	F	Charlton Horethorne	Home	8	0	" 8	Y	Charlton United	Home		
" 19	B	Wincanton Town	Home	13	1	" 8	F	Charlton Horethorne	Away		
" 19	F	R.N.A.S. Yeovilton	Away	3	13	" 15	B	Wincanton Town	Away		
" 26	Y	Sparkford & Queen Camel Utd.	Away	5	3	" 15					
" 26	F	~~Sexey's School, Bruton~~	~~Home~~			" 22	Y	Odcombe	Home		
Nov. 2	Y	Stoke-under-Ham	Away	1	2	" 22	B	~~Cheriton~~	Away		
" 2	F	~~Bruton Athletic~~	~~Home~~			Mar. 1		2nd Round McCreery Cup			
" 9	Y	Ash Rovers	Home	2	2	" 8	Y	St. John's Gym, Yeovil	Home		
" 9	F	~~Templecombe~~	~~Away~~			" 15	Y	Montacute	Away		
" 16	×	2nd Rd. Merthyr Guest Cup				" 22	Y	Hambridge & Westport Utd.	Home		
" 23	Y	Keinton Mandeville	Home	5	3	" 29	B	Templecombe Athletic HOME	~~Away~~		
" ~~16~~ 23		CHERITON	AWAY	4	3	April 4	B	(G. Fri.) ~~Templecombe Athletic~~	Home		
" ~~23~~ 30	Y	~~Yeovil Baptists~~ EVERCREECH	Home	3	3	" 5	B	Alweston	Away		
" 30	F	~~Wincanton Town~~	~~Away~~			" 5		~~Wincanton Town~~	~~Home~~		
Dec. 7	Y	Charlton United	Away	2	2	" 7	Y	Stoke-under-Ham	Away		
" 7	F	Sexey's School, Bruton	Away	2	5	" 12	Y	Ash Rovers	Away		
" 14	B	Wincanton Town (Blackmore Vale Charity Cup)	Home	12	0	" 19	B	~~Alweston~~	Home		
" 14						" 26	Y	Milborne Port	Home		
" 21	Y	~~Bradford Abbas~~	~~Away~~			May 3	B	~~Cheriton~~	Home		

Y. Yeovil & District League.   B. Blackmore Vale League.   F. Friendly.

Football Club Fixtures Card, 1946-47.

Ansford Rovers football team, 1953. *Left to right, front row:* John Parham; Bert Lodge; Ted Ranger; Norman Stone; Bob Hedditch. *Back row:* Alf Chivers; French Chivers; John Harrison; Bert Woods; Ivan Parsons; Alex Chambers; Ern Chivers; M. Helps. *(photo L. Veryard)*

Castle Cary Association Football Club with the seven cups won in the season 1959-60. *Left to right, front row:* W. Allen; K. Hoddinott; R. Parsons; D. Patten; B. Rowe; J. Stokes. *Back row:* L. King; G. Kingdom; N. Francis; D. Loxton; G. Graham; L. Veryard; D. Brookes; R. Pitman; D. Stickland; R. Dycer; H. Pitman; R. Close. *(photo L. Veryard)*

CASTLE CARY RUGBY UNION FOOTBALL CLUB

Castle Cary R.U.F.C. was established in 1888, with their first match, a draw, against Shepton Mallet on 1st December 1888, in the Clothier brothers' field at Ansford, watched by a crowd of about 60. Club headquarters was at the George Hotel, and a permanent ground was laid out at Catherine's Close. The first President was John S. Donne and Captain was John O. Cash.

By the 1889/90 season they had been nicknamed "The Chickens", a sobriquet they retained for many years. In 1897 a grandstand was constructed to hold 100 spectators; entry was 3d per head, ladies free, but was demolished by a gale in 1899. With the outbreak of the Great War the Club disbanded and was only resurrected in 1921, when games were played at Millbrook Field. By 1938 the level of support was insufficient to raise a team and the Club again disbanded, but was revived in 1952 under the leadership of Paul Greenough and Peter Trickey, with headquarters at the Rink building of the Britannia Hotel, and a pitch opposite West Park on Mr. Kynaston's land. Increasing suppport eventually enabled the Club to purchase a site near the Brook House Inn where it has built a Clubhouse next to its pitch.

Castle Cary R.U.F.C. for the season 1893/4. *Front row, from left:* A. Apsey; G. Coleman; J. Cutler; C. Cave.
Middle row, from left: F. M. Tabor; J. M. Green; J. O. Cash (Captain); J. S. Donne (President); F. Ovens; W. A. Bord; A. Sharman.
Back row, from left: A. Harrold (Hon. Sec.); C. Cooper; W. B. Mackie; J. H. Mackie; J. H. Mackie; J. Mackie; G. Hill; W. S. Donne.
(photo P. Fletcher)

Castle Cary R.U.F.C. for the season 1975/6. *Front row, from left:* Steve Armson; Dave Hoddinott; Dave Price; William Hole (Captain); Richard Slaney. *Back row, from left:* Geoff Crang; Bert Farthing; Martin Flower; Clive Snell; John Shaw; David Boyer; Nick Ollie; John Bradley; Howard Bamping; Richard Crang; Bob Fry. *(photo P. Fletcher)*

CYCLING

Jack Pike, the well-known proprietor of a cycle shop by the Horse Pond, was also a highly successful competitor in the sport. He is seen here, on the right, with his astonishing array of prizes and trophies, in the 1920s. Charlie Pike is on the left.
(photo B. Lush)

SKITTLES

The "Magnificent Eight" skittles team in 1970, league champions at the Constitutional Club for several years, where the photograph was taken. *Left to right, front row:* Ern Baby; Roger Otton; Vic Higgins. *Back row:* John Veryard; Ken Ward; Brian Harris; Alan Biddiscombe; Tony Perret. *(photo R. Otton)*

DARTS

Dart playing friends at the Waggon and Horses in the 1960s. *From left:* Ern Chivers; Ted Lindup; Bert Lodge; Harry Read. *(photo Ruth Lodge)*

TABLE TENNIS

The Table Tennis Club thrived during the 1950s and is seen here in the Constitutional Club as Champions. *Front row, from left:* Sarah Barrett; Queenie Pagram; Mrs "Jimmie" Humpries; Major St. John Whitehead; Mrs L. Kynaston; Mrs B. White; Mrs Sparkes (Steward). *Back row, from left:* Bert White; Dick Darby; Dick Hunt; Ralph Eglen; Robert Foote; Ray Boyer; Clive Chambers; Len Humpries; Norman White; NK; Charlie Chambers; Ernie Oborne; Les Kynaston; John Mainstone; George ?; Gerry Amor; Maurice White; Len Close. (photo Ray Boyer)

EVENTS

Considerable excitement was clearly engendered by the landing of this R.M.Y. Biplane at Millbrook, on 15 June 1916. The first aircraft to fly over Castle Cary was in August 1912, and during the 1930s the Merrick brothers built their own plane behind their shop in "The Triangle".

PASTORAL PLAYS

Castle Cary Literary Society was founded on 19th October 1904 as a reading circle for literary study. It was found that dramatic readings were very much more interesting than any other kind and Shakespeare became the favourite author. Performance in costume of scenes from Shakespearian plays followed and were such a success that the members felt justified in attempting the play "As You Like It" in a much more public and ambitious manner in the grounds of Castle Cary Vicarage in 1907.

The standards of production, costumes and scale of events performed by the society have never since been equalled in Cary; four more plays being staged before the Great War brought an end to the productions; namely "A Midsummer Night's Dream" in 1908; "The Merchant of Venice" in 1909; "Twelfth Night" in 1912; and "Much Ado About Nothing" in 1914.

An indication of the scale of these productions can be illustrated by the example of "A Midsummer Night's Dream", which had a combined cast and orchestra performing Mendelssohn score of about 70 persons. A grandstand was erected on the Vicarage lawn to seat 500, and rows of seats and chairs provided room for a further 700. Special trains were laid on to bring members of the audience from a wide area.

The cast of "A Midsummer Night's Dream" performed on 23rd July 1908 with Mr. T. S. Donne as "Egeus"; Mr. C. Pither as "Theseus"; Mr. Harold Pither as "Oberon"; Mr. Hugh Pitman as "Puck" and an entire cast of Caryites. *(photo A. V. Pearse)*

Mr. R. W. Martin, who also played the part of "Pyramus", is shown here in his costume as "Bottom", showing the attention to detail displayed by these productions. *(photo A. V. Pearse)*

"The Merchant of Venice" was performed on 8th July 1909, with Mr. Charles Pither as "Shylock"; Mr. John Pither as "Bassanio"; and Miss Martin as "Portia". Illumination of the Vicarage grounds during the evening added to the atmosphere of the performance. *(photo K. Wright)*

The cast of "Twelfth Night" performed on 4th July 1912 in the Vicarage grounds, including Mrs. C. C. Martin as "Olivia"; Mrs. R. W. Martin as "Sebastian"; Mr. C. Pither as "Sir Andrew Aguecheek"; Mr. J. Pither as the "Duke of Orsino" and Mr. H. J. Pudden as "Malvolio". *(photo A. V. Pearse)*

An early photograph of the Town Band from 1907. *Front row, left to right:* H. G. Day; NK; Herbert Biggin; A. Creed. *Middle row, left to right:* Alfred Cooper; Charles Cooper; Herbert Farrant; George Weeks; NK; William Cooper: *Back row, left to right:* NK; W. Roper; Percy Vallis. A temperance festival in 1893 had provided the impetus to establish a band, and over £35 was raised by an appeal to equip one, which had its first public appearance at Hadspen House. However, some members were not as enthusiastic supporters of the temperance movement as others and two sections of the band emerged, the "abstainers" and the "moderates". The two elements did not work comfortably together, so in 1897 it was decided to drop the title of Temperance and become the Town Band. The Band became very popular, reaching its peak membership in the 1920s. *(photo R. Howard)*

A view of the laying of the stone commemorating the construction of the Church Room - "This stone was laid by the Rt. Hon. Henry Hobhouse, 20 July 1933". In the background are the "Swiss" cottages, almshouses built in 1881 on the site of the Parish Pound at the expense of Miss Meade.

The Church Room was built in 1933 by Theodore Rossiter of Ansford and his son Ralph. Pictured here with the foundation stone are: *left to right:* NK; NK; NK; Arthur Rossiter; Ralph Rossiter; NK; Theodore Rossiter and his wife Annie.
(photo Mrs C. Rossiter)

Castle Cary celebrated George V's Coronation on 22 June 1911 with a day of events throughout the town. The local M.P., Mr. Ernest Jardine, presented 221 children with Post Office savings accounts of 1s 0d, and Mrs. J. S. Donne provided souvenir books for 385 children. There were church and chapel services, a public luncheon and tea for children and old folks. The photograph shows the gathering in The Market Place, which took place at 10 a.m. with the F. Co., 4th Batt. The Prince Albert's Somerset L.I., the school children and the Coronation Committee. The National Anthem and other patriotic songs were sung, and as shown, the F. Co., fired a "feu de joi". Events such as this show Castle Cary at the peak of its prosperity in the years leading up to the Great War. *(photo B. Laver)*

A rare, if not unique, survival from the 1911 Coronation festivities is this copy of the Programme for the musical entertainment. Prominent amongst the performances were selections by the Church Institute Coons, a photograph of whom has also been preserved *(opposite, top)*. Present are Messrs. C. Bellringer; G. Bolson; E. Dill; G. Dill; J. Fox; B. Hall; W. Newport; H. Pitman; J. Pitman. The Coons were formed in 1902 to participate in the celebrations marking the Coronation of Edward VII and very popular in the town and surrounding district. *(photo J. Sweet)*

East Somerset General Election, 1910.

THE FAVOUR OF
YOUR VOTE AND INTEREST
Is respectfully solicited on behalf of
Mr. ERNEST JARDINE.
Printed and Published by Bennett Brothers Ltd., Bristol.

The East Somerset Presentation to Ernest Jardine Esq. M.P. June 1911.

Ernest Jardine was a flamboyant character who made quite an impact in Somerset. A Nottinghamshire manufacturer, his local interests included ownership of a textile machine mill at Shepton Mallet, and acquisition of the ruins of Glastonbury Abbey, to facilitate their transfer to the Church of England in 1909. He stood as Unionist candidate for East Somerset in the two General Elections held during 1910 and was victorious in both. A Unionist Fete was held on Whit Monday, 1911, at Florida House, where a spectacular array of silver plate was presented to him, to which over 7,000 had subscribed. In addition to a large silver vase surmounted by a figure of "Victory" there were four ornate flower bowls. Each piece was inscribed "Presented to Ernest Jardine Esq. M.P., by his friends in East Somerset, as a mark of esteem, June 5th 1911". A Coronation Oak was also planted.
(photos A. V. Pearse)

Several Caryites were on board the R.M.S. Titanic when it sank on April 15th 1912 off Cape Race, the greatest maritime disaster in history. H. J. Pitman of Castle Cary was Third Officer on the liner. Aged 34, he had been sixteen years in the mercantile marine, and served in the Blue Anchor Line until joining the White Star Company in 1908. He had enjoyed a holiday in Castle Cary before leaving to take up his appointment on the Titanic, having been Third Officer on the "Oceanic". As the liner foundered Mr. Pitman was sent by First Officer Murdock in charge of lifeboat 5, with forty passengers and five of the crew. It would have held more, but no women could be found at the time it was lowered. Tied to boat 5 was boat 7, one of those that contained few people. Officer Pitman and the boats in his charge were later rescued by the "Carpathia". Less fortunate were the Herman family. Sam Herman was for many years a butcher in Castle Cary, and also for some years proprietor of the "Britannia Hotel" and was travelling with his wife and two daughters to join a brother of Mrs. Herman's in the States. A lad named George Sweet, aged 15, who worked with Mr. Herman, was with them, and both he and his employer perished with the vessel. Mrs. Herman and her daughters survived. *(photo Castle Cary Visitor, May 1912)*

WOMEN'S INSTITUTE

Castle Cary Women's Institute was formed on 29th May 1922, with Ansford being included in the title since 1945. Miss Mabel Woodforde was the first President, a role which she fulfilled for 23 years. Meetings, normally held in the Methodist schoolroom, were fairly formal, and a register was kept of those attending committee meetings. In addition to guest speakers, cookery and needlework were prominent activities. Much work was done for charitable causes, including the growing and sending of vegetables to local hospitals. Committee members were also responsible by rotation, and normally in pairs, for staging a social half-hour to conclude meetings, and were often very enterprising in their selections.

Throughout the 1920s and 30s the W.I. was well known in the district for the series of plays, mostly Shakespearean, which it performed in the Town Hall. Production was normally organized by Miss Woodforde, and members spent much time rehearsing and preparing costumes. Members also performed the male parts. Notable productions were "Much Ado About Nothing" in 1930; "Twelfth Night" in 1931; "The Merchant of Venice" in 1932; "The Merry Wives of Windsor" in 1934 and "A Midsummer Night's Dream" in 1938.

During the war, members concentrated on helping the war effort. They continued to make jam, in spite of problems acquiring the ingredients, and managed 871 lbs. in 1941. They rolled bandages, made camouflage netting at South Court, and knitted items for the troops, as well as disseminating advice relating to prudent use of scarce resources. In spite of wartime conditions, members staged "Twelfth Night" in 1942; "She Stoops to Conquer" in 1943 and "School for Scandal" in 1944.

The milestone of 100 members was achieved in 1946, and the Silver Jubilee of the Institute was celebrated in 1947; the Golden Jubilee in 1972 and Diamond Jubilee in 1982. A tree was planted at Caryford Hall to celebrate the 75th Anniversary in 1997.

The cast of a Shakespearian play outside the Post Office during the 1930s. Miss Mabel Woodforde is on the extreme left, and the performers include: *front row, left;* Madge Barrett; Peggy Dodd. *(photo A. V. Pearse)*

Members of the Castle Cary and Ansford W.I., who presented scenes from "The Merry Wives of Windsor" in the preliminary round of the County W.I. Drama Festival at West Pennard Village Hall, during the 1960s. Included are: Mrs. Dunford; Beryl Francis; Joyce Weeks; Katherine Rathbone (with recorder); Dorothy James; Marjorie White; and Mrs. Aubertin. *(photo B. Laver)*

Considerable effort went into the decoration of Fore Street for the celebration of the Silver Jubilee of King George V and Queen Mary in 1935. *(photo Mrs. M. Dunn)*

The Queen and Prince Phillip at Castle Cary station en route to the Bath and West Show, 3rd June 1966. *(photo Mrs. Churchouse)*

Staff, with families and friends on an outing to Weymouth awaiting embarkation at Jonathan Cruse and Gass's Clanville Sawmills in 1948.

Ansford Secondary School participated in the 1954 All England Schools Athletic Championships held 16th - 17th July, as part of the Somerset Team. Ansford Team Leader John Harrison is seen kneeling, extreme left, second row. Ansford winners included: *back row second from left*: R. Grounds who ran 440 yards in 51.7 secs.; *front row, fifth from left*: Vivian Bradley, javelin, 104 feet; *and third row from front, third from left*: D. Luke, senior boys' high jump 6 feet ½ inch. *(photo Mrs. P. Harrison)*

FLOWER SHOWS AND THE CASTLE CARY GARDENING ASSOCIATION

Flower Shows have a long history in Castle Cary. The first attempt to stage one was in 1889 in connection with the Y.M.C.A., at the Town Hall, with John Boyd as President. A larger show was held in 1890. Other organizations adopted the idea, such as the Temperance Society and the Women's Institute and during the 1930s the Bible Class founded by John Pither started to organize shows of garden produce. After the war, seeds donated by the American Government became available, distributed in this area by M. H. Milner of Weston-super-Mare. It was decided to hold a show in a tent on the Recreation Ground on 25th August 1949, displaying fruit, flowers and vegetables; the event being combined with a children's gymkhana, and an annual series thus commenced. Later the Scout hut, Constitutional Club, Drill Hall and Ansford School became show venues. Stalwarts during this period were Mr.and Mrs. G. Yeabsley, J. Pike and Police Constable G. Laver.

The Flower Shows continue to attract enthusiastic participants.

The Flower Show of 1951 held by the Castle Cary and District British Legion, together with side shows and sports, and a Trade Show by Castle Cary Chamber of Commerce was held in the Donald Pither Memorial Field on 23rd August. The winners are amongst: *left to right:* Bill May; Geoff Laver; Hubert Laver; Grace Yeabsley; Mrs. W. Pike; J. R. Bulley; Jack Pike; George Yeabsley; Len Joslin; Ernie Hunt; Olive Thomas; Percy Thomas; Lady Parsons. *(photo B.Laver)*

Jack Pike is here being presented with a cup during the 1960s. *Left to right:* P. Thomas; Mrs.O. Thomas; Jack Pike; J. R. Bulley; G. Yeabsley; NK; PC G. Laver; E. Hunt; NK; Mr. Joslin. *(photo Mrs. G. Ruddle)*

Castle Cary Flower Show Cup presentation in the 1960s. *Left to right:* Mrs. Yeabsley; Janet Hutchfield; Bill Stride; Harold Garrett; NK; Geoff Laver; Paul Sherrell; Mrs. Thomas. *(photo Mrs. G. Ruddle)*

The Gardening Club Flower Show at the Drill Hall 1964/65. *(photo Gardening Club)*

CASTLE CARY CHOIR

The Castle Cary Choir was founded in 1965 by David Vaux with the inital purpose of entertaining the 350 people attending the annual Harvest Super at Ansford School. Having met with a rapturous reception the group decided to stay together and hold regular rehearsals enabling them to assist religious and charitable institutions raise money by giving concerts.

Since those early days the Choir has gone from strength to strength and presently consists of a mixed voice ensemble of 50 - 60 members presenting a varied repertoire of sacred and secular music, including folk, spiritual and modern items. The Choir gives about eight concerts a year in Somerset and neighbouring counties and has enjoyed considerable success at competitive festivals: in 1987 it won five classes, and the trophy for Best Choir, at the Mid-Somerset Festival at Bath, and in 1989 was the only Somerset Choir to reach the finals of the Six Counties Choir of the West competition held in Sherborne.

Highlights in its programme have been giving a concert at the Guards Chapel, London, together with the Band of the Welsh Guards, and also at the Royal Star and Garter Home at Richmond, and with the Blues and Royals in Worthing. The Choir also visits France occasionally and gives concerts in Remelard, the twin town of Castle Cary and Ansford.

David Vaux, the founder conductor, handed over the baton to Ivor Chainey in 1976, who remained musical director until his death in March 2000. The Choir is now under the direction of Dorothy Hann and includes founder members Beth Ashman and Audrey Parry.

Founder members of the Castle Cary Choir singing Christmas carols in the Market Place, 1965. *(photo Mrs. A. Parry)*

The Choir pictured in 1984 having just won two silver cups in the Open and Sacred Choral section of the Mid-Somerset Festival at Bath. *(photo Mrs. A. Parry)*

CASTLE CARY YOUTH CLUB

Members of Castle Cary Youth Club performing a play in the 1940s. *Left to right:* Mr. H. T. Gough; John Hart; Jean Asher; Derek Hutchfield; Hazel Stokes; Vera Creed. *(photo Mrs. P. Harrison)*

CARY AMATEUR THEATRICAL SOCIETY

C.A.T.S. was formed in the late 1970s and have presented a show, normally a musical, at Ansford School almost annually, including "The Boyfriend", "Annie" and "The Sound of Music".

In 1996 C.A.T.S. produced "My Fair Lady". Seen here are the entire cast, including Roger Bull as Alfred P. Doolittle (in morning suit), with his daughter Sarah as Eliza Doolittle (standing beside him wearing hat). The show was directed by Lee Mosley and the musical director was Mark Tromans. *(photo R. Bull)*

THE CASTLE CARY PLAYERS

During the 1950s the Castle Cary Players established themselves as a group performing an annual pantomime, and in 1955 adopted a constitution confirming the practice of an annual production and establishing that donations from any profits arising from such productions be devoted to the support of Castle Cary parish church or to the other churches in Castle Cary and Ansford. Performances were held on three successive nights at Ansford Secondary Modern School, and for one night during the following week at North Cadbury Village Hall.

In 1957 the Castle Cary Players produced T. E. D. Lewis's "The Sleeping Beauty"; the photograph shows the cast, musicians and stage hands. The principal boy and girl were Beryl Francis and Brenda Cornish, with other regular members in the cast including Graham Asher, Roy Talbot, Gerry Toms and Jack Sweet. Costumes were made by Doris Trowbridge and Gwen Helps, and musical accompaniment was provided by Tom Trowbridge and May Youings on pianos and George Gower on drums. In the front, centre, is Ken Youings, who adapted and produced the show. *(photo Mrs. V. Nicholls)*

Periodically an "Old English Market" is held in the town with shopkeepers encouraged to wear an appropriate costume. Brian Lush of Lush Butchers is seen here in 1991 selling his pies from a hundred year old barrow boy's cart originally from Covent Garden. *(photo B. Lush)*

CARNIVALS

During the 19th century, and probably earlier, parades were held in Castle Cary to celebrate a variety of events such as Feast days, or an occasion of particular importance to some club or society, and increasingly these were accompanied by the Temperance and later the Town band. An annual Carnival was established in 1919 to celebrate the return of war veterans, which consisted of decorated floats and vehicles, often produced by various tradesmen or businesses, as well as the band and individuals in costume. The 1922 carnival was a particularly ambitious undertaking, with considerable ingenuity in the design of the floats. The run of Carnivals continued until the depression in the 1930s.

November 1945 saw the revival of Carnivals by the Welcome Home Committee to raise funds for returning service personnel but fuel shortages and the lack of people to organize the events were major problems compounded by the tragedy of a stray firework setting light to the firework store on a lorry, which exploded in 1947, ending the revival after an all too short run in 1950.

The modern Carnivals were started in 1977 to celebrate Jubilee Year and are held on the second Saturday evening in October and feature many walkers and decorated floats - the emphasis being on bright lights, brilliant costumes and loud music. Many thousands of pounds are raised for charity.

The spirit which promoted the series of Comrades carnivals is captured in this view of some individual costumes from 1922. In addition to the "injured" soldier and sailor are a signpost, organ grinder and monkey. *(photo A. V. Pearse)*

The "Cary Comrades Carnival" held on 11th August 1922, the third annual event held after the Great War, was a very ambitious spectacle commencing with a procession past the church to Millbrook Field, where the numerous decorated vehicles and individual characters assembled. Many of the costumes were very original in design; shown here are the staff from the Barrett grocery and bakery shops, with a giant bottle made by W. R. H. Barrett to represent a Gilbey's product, to the left, and from Ralph Otton's furnishing business to the right. *(photo A. V. Pearse)*

Comrades Carnival 1922 – A float representing the League of Nations.

During the afternoon of 11th August 1922 all the entries assembled in South Cary and paraded to Millbrook Field. Most of the decorated floats were built on prams, bicycles, motor bikes and side-cars. *(photos by Mrs Clothier)*

Top Left – Muriel Firth, winner of a cake stand and First Prize in Children's Section.
Bottom left – Decorated Motorcycle and sidecar.
Bottom right – Mr. and Mrs. Firth, winners of a shaving mirror.

Carnival floats were often very inventive, as seen in this tonsorial parlour portrayed in one of the Comrades Carnivals of the 1920s. *(photo A. V. Pearse)*

Carnival time in the 1930s produced this appropriate float from C. H. Thomas & Sons. Pictured near the parish church with the horse are George Hoare and Arthur Rapson, Frank Sweetman and Harry Barber are at the window, and John Thomas Snr. stands in the doorway, while Albert Cutler attends to the roof. At the rear of the float are Albert Wilton and Jack Firth.
(photo Mrs M. Clothier)

The "Squatters" Removal Band entry in the 1946 carnival, the first held after the war. *Left to right:* Albert Howard; Albert Wilton; Ewart King; Tom Goodland (in chair); Mrs. Fry; Ern Meadon; Ken Clothier; J. Fry; Donald Ranger.
(photo K. Clothier)

The 1946 Carnival Queen and her Attendants. *Left to right, Front row:* Vera Creed; Elfreda Perkins; Paddy Marks.
Back row: Betty Corbett, nee Smart; Joan Francis (The Queen); Jean Chambers. This was only the second carnival held after the war, the procession consisted of six bands and about thirty decorated floats with fifty Ansford School boys as torch bearers. The following year due to petrol shortage the carnival was postponed and a firework display was to be held. At the commencement the fireworks went off with one big bang! In 1950 due to lack of interest carnivals were abandoned.
(photo Mrs E. Moore)

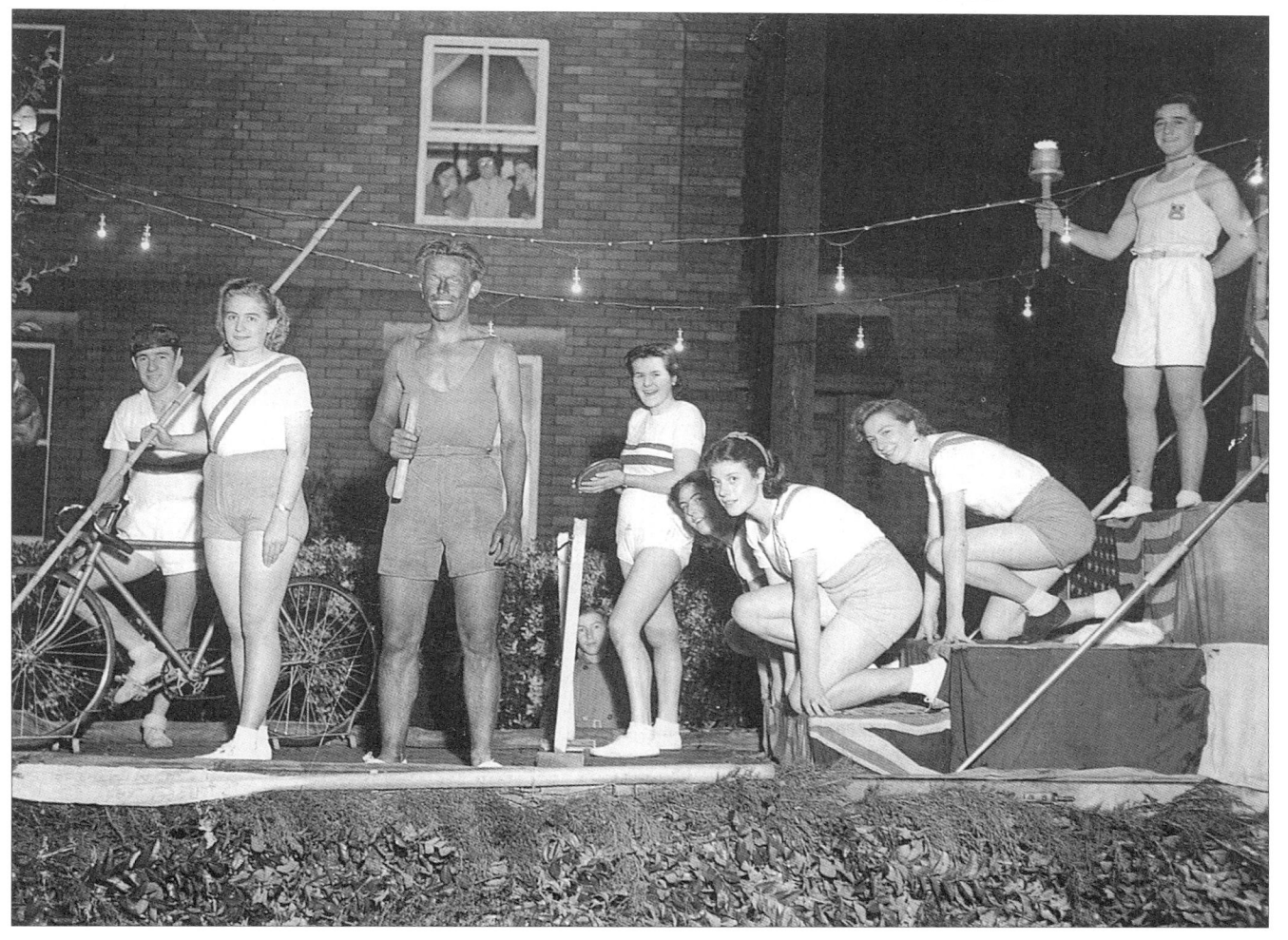

The Olympic Games 1948 by Castle Cary Youth Club. Participants - *Left to right:* Ted Lush; Vera Creed; Stan Vervard; Janet Lush; Betty Yeabsley; Penny Pitman; Brenda Francis; Graham Asher. *(photo Janet Hutchfield)*

The Happy Workers 1986 – Carnival float construction at Orchard Farm by Alan Mullett, Gordon Stockman, Chris Booker and Chief Electrician Len Fennon who was still attending carnivals in his 90th year. *(photo R. Boyer)*

Brighton Belles Cary Comedians 1980 – This was the fourth year in carnival for the comedians and the float was built on a fourteen foot long farm trailer. Lighting was by a 2kW generator carried on the tractor. Members on board were from left to right: Angie Hughes, Sue Stockman, Mo Higgins, Sue Leach, Jan Hutchfield, Martin Flower and Tony Hallet.

Cary Crackpots with their Playgroup entry from the early 1990s. *From left, front row:* June Wake; Angela Helps; Hazel Warren; Diana Pinnions; Dawn Vincent. *Back row:* Millie King; Mary Edwards; Marilyn Burridge; Sara Alford; Sylvia Francis; Lesley Hill; Gilly Reeves; Janet Barker; Pauline Handford. *(photo Lesley Hill)*

Cary Comedians 1998 – County Comic Class Winners entitled "Yer Tis, Speedy Gonzales". On board (from the front) are Louise Cleal; Reggie Eggleton; Mark Darby; Caroline Evans; Marie Eggleton; Ray Boyer; Jean Spearpoint; Sandy Millard; Carol Chivers; Angela Mackinnon; Olive Boyer; Sue Stockman; Mo Higgins; Gordon Stockman. 21 years after their formation Cary Comedians won their first County Cup with this 85 feet long display of colour and lights. *(photo R. Boyer)*

The Britannia Carnival Club produced a magnificently spectacular entry in the 1999 season "Out of Africa" which competed successfully against the formidable productions seen in the County circuit. *(photo Britannia Carnival Club)*

CURIOSITIES

ONE MILE TO CASTLE CARY.

This is mile-little game down here at Castle Cary.

Fresh from the decorous days of Edwardian courtship comes this colourful example of a postcard published by Birn Brothers of London, one of the standard 'milepost' design (series 2452) produced in Germany and overprinted for sale in many different places. *(photo B. Lush)*

A selection from the extensive range of Castle Cary souvenir and crested china manufactured prior to the First World War. Cary crested china was mainly manufactured by the Arcadian company of Stoke-on-Trent, though examples have been found made by Ford and Pointon and Grosvenor Ware. Many pieces, although unmarked, are clearly by Arcadian, and sometimes bear the retailer's mark "C. Pither and Son, Castle Cary". Well over 30 different designs of Cary crested china have been noted. Even more interesting are the larger items of Cary china which appear to have been produced in extensive ranges, often decorated with a representation of the church. These beautiful pieces are very rare and collectable today. A selection can be viewed in the Museum, together with earthenware items inscribed for various grocers, etc, trading in the town.
(A. V. Pearse and B. Lush collection)

Modern Castle Cary souvenir wares include mugs produced to show the Round House and Market House, both issued in the 1990s, and a mug designed to commemorate the Millennium. *(A. V. Pearse collection, photo B. Lush)*

The first decade of the twentieth century saw the beginnings of powered flight. The first aeroplane passed over Castle Cary in 1912, and postcard publishers were keen to exploit "aero-mania". Unfortunately the cameras of the period could not satisfactorily capture fast moving objects like aircraft and therefore they were drawn on master copies, which were then reproduced. Here we have a view of the Market Place with added aeroplane on a card post-marked 1913. *(photo A. V. Pearse)*

During 1999 several tunnels were discovered beneath the surface of the field opposite South Cary House in South Street. As the photograph shows, a passage has been cut through the natural sandstone and roofed with flags. Their purpose is unknown, and full extent undetermined. Similar discoveries were made in 1910/11 when a tunnel 24 feet in length and covered in part by a brick arch was revealed beneath the back offices of South Cary House, and a further tunnel was discovered in the field, as above, as a result of subsidence, of which the present discovery may represent a re-opening. Tradition suggests their former use for smuggling, but it is reasonable to suggest a more prosaic origin.
(photo P. Brewin)

A Martin's Stores glass from the 1930s. *(photo B. Lush collection)*

Another Birn Brother's card, overprinted for Castle Cary, c1908. *(A. V. pearse collection)*

Photographs fail to capture the intricacy of the Roman bronze figurine of a Lar - a household deity - discovered in 1999 during work on the "Castle Rise" development at Manor Farm. Many Roman houses, especially of higher status, possessed a small household shrine, or small room set aside for this purpose. The Castle Cary example was found in a disused lime-kiln; perhaps placed there as a part of some ritual. The springs nearby from which the River Cary rises may have been a focus for spiritual activity and it is likely that a substantial Roman building existed in this vicinity, perhaps obliterated by construction of the castle or development of the town.
(photo J&D Churchhouse)

Situated on the wall above the post-box at Lower Ansford, the stone carved beast is a grotesque originally from the ruins of Glastonbury Abbey and installed in its present position in the late 1930s by W. J. Barrett, assisted by local builder George Stockley. The weather vane mounted above was recovered from the ruins of the Ansford manor house nearby. *(photo A. V. Pearse)*

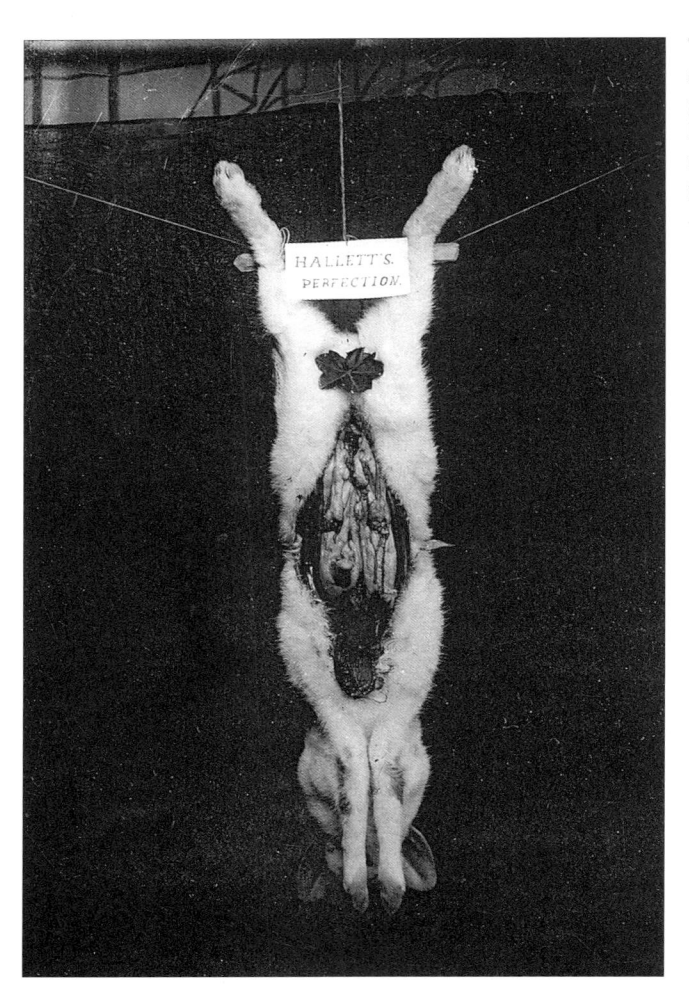

The most curious image to emerge in the search for material for the book is this photograph of a rabbit, labelled "HALLETT'S PERFECTION" taken from a glass plate negative of about 1890. An explanation of its purpose has yet to emerge. *(photo N. Foster)*

The title page from a book dated 1800 by a previously unknown Castle Cary author, designed for use, which may mean that it is the only copy still in existence. The oldest item in this collection, it shows that Castle Cary can still provide many unexpected surprises.
(A. V. Pearse collection)

THE

PERSIAN DIARY;

OR,

REFLECTION'S ORIENTAL GIFT

OF

DAILY COUNSEL

———————

———— Thy silver days were scattered o'er with flowers of fragrant virtues, every morning gathered by the rising of the sun, and not a song of any bird addressed thine ear, but brought a note to excellence.

Nature in all her loveliness thy tutor. With gentle spirit, and a bosom pure, thy calm attention listened to her counsel; where by the fountain's side, or on the hill, she taught the daily precept.

This made thee, SELIMA, so amiable.

———————

BY WILLIAM ROBSON,

OF CASTLE CARY.

London:
PRINTED FOR THE AUTHOR,
By W. Wilson, St. Peter's Hill, Doctors' Commons;
And sold by J. Wallis, Pater-noster Row; and J. Hatchard, Piccadilly.
Entered at Stationers' Hall.
1800

FURTHER READING

MEMORIES OF CASTLE CARY AND ANSFORD. The Living History Group (Dickins Printers 1998) 179p. A collection of reminiscences about life in the two communities during much of the twentieth century. Illustrated. Reaches parts that other books do not.

CASTLE CARY, NORTH CADBURY AND WINCANTON. Sam Miller and Bridget Laver (Chalford 1997) 128p. A good selection of photographs with captions by two indefatigable local historians.

CASTLE CARY FROM OLD PHOTOGRAPHS. Patrick Dunion (Fox Publications 1983) 36p. An interesting selection with brief captions. Out of print, but copies can be found occasionally.

THE CASTLE CARY VISITOR. A monthly periodical issued from 1896 to 1915 and edited by William Macmillan from 1896 to 1911 and by his children 1912 to 1915. An astonishing fund of information on multitudinous aspects of the Castle Cary area and its history, with occasional illustrations. Normally available in bound volumes minus the advertisement pages, in some local libraries. Individual monthly issues and odd volumes can occasionally be found but are very rare.

THE VISITOR. A current monthly publication containing occasional articles on aspects of Castle Cary and neighbourhood.

CASTLE CARY. Michael McGarvie (Avalon Industries 1980). 48p. Subtitled "A sketch of its industrial and social history with special reference to Boyd's hair factory". Erudite and informative, with good illustrations.

SOMERSET FOLK GUIDES - CASTLE CARY AND DISTRICT. (Folk Press 1925). 50p. Concise, with illustrations, maps and advertisements. Very rare indeed.

HISTORIC TOWNS IN SOMERSET - ARCHAEOLOGY AND PLANNING. Michael Aston and Roger Leach (Craggs. 1977). Contains a brief overview of Castle Cary, with maps.

HISTORICAL NOTES ON CASTLE CARY. Rev. A. W. Grafton (W. Bentley 1890) 23p. Mostly concerned with the parish church, and also a list of important dates.

THE CASTLES OF CARY. Cyril P. Hershon (Pavalas Press 1990). 96p. A comprehensive account of aspects of the castle and its history; contains a reprint of the P.S.A.N.H.S. article of 1890 on the castle excavations.

KELLY'S DIRECTORY OF SOMERSETSHIRE. Issued at approximately five yearly intervals from 1860 to 1939, and containing short historical descriptions of Castle Cary and Ansford, etc, and lists of private residents and tradespeople.

DIARY OF PARSON JAMES WOODFORDE. The Ansford diary has been issued by the Parson Woodforde Society in two volumes, ed. R. L. Winstanley (1977 and 1980). A five volume edition, ed. John Beresford was published by Oxford University Press 1924 - 1931, and there are also several single volume selections of extracts. Essential reading to capture the atmosphere of this period.

PROCEEDINGS OF THE SOMERSET ARCHAEOLOGICAL AND NATURAL HISTORY SOCIETY. There are several articles on Castle Cary including an account of the excavation of Cary Castle in Vol. 36, 1890, and historical notes on the town in Vol 16, 1870.

CASTLE CARY PAST AND PRESENT EXHIBITION. Souvenir Magazine (1974). Contains much useful information.

HISTORY AND ANTIQUITIES OF THE COUNTY OF SOMERSET. John Collinson (1791) 3 vols. The first detailed historical description of Castle Cary and Ansford.

SOMERSETSHIRE DELINEATED. C. and J. Greenwood (1821). Useful facts, including; "Castle Cary ... containing 299 inhabited houses, and 333 families, 158 of whom are employed in agriculture, 167 in trade, manufacture, or handicraft, and 8 not included in either class ... The country around Castle Cary is extremely beautiful, and the society in the town and neighbourhood is highly respectable, which with the convenience of its situation, renders it a place of agreeable retirement." "Ansford ... containing 48 inhabited houses and 54 families, whereof 25 are employed in agriculture. The church consists of a nave only, with a tower and three bells ..."

HISTORY AND ANTIQUITIES OF THE COUNTY OF SOMERSET. Rev. William Phelps (1836).

GENERAL VIEW OF THE AGRICULTURE OF THE COUNTY OF SOMERSET. John Billingsley (1795). The agricultural context at the dawn of the agricultural revolution.